MY FIRST LITTLE BOOK OF INTERSECTIONAL ACTIVISM

MY FIRST LITTLE BOOK OF INTERSECTIONAL ACTIVISM

Titania McGrath

CONSTABLE

CONSTABLE

First published in Great Britain in 2020 by Constable

1 3 5 7 9 10 8 6 4 2

Copyright © Titania McGrath, 2020
Illustrations by Emil Dacanay
Graphs by Liane Payne

The moral right of the author has been asserted.

A CIP catalogue record for this book
is available from the British Library.

ISBN: 978-1-47213-427-1 (hardback)

Typeset in Sabon LT by Hewer Text UK Ltd, Edinburgh
Printed and bound in Great Britain by Clays Ltd, Elcograf S.p.A.

Papers used by Constable are from well-managed
forests and other responsible sources.

Constable
An imprint of
Little, Brown Book Group
Carmelite House
50 Victoria Embankment
London EC4Y 0DZ

An Hachette UK Company
www.hachette.co.uk

www.littlebrown.co.uk

I believe the children are our future,
teach them well and let them lead the way.

Whitney Houston

CONTENTS

My First Little Book of Intersectional Activism

INTRODUCTION

This is a book for aspiring activists between the ages of six months and six years. If you're an adult, kindly fuck off and read something else.

Now that ancient prying eyes have been averted, we may speak candidly. As a young person, you represent the next generation of intersectional warrior queens. I make no apologies for using advanced terminology such as 'intersectional', because I refuse to patronise you in the way your parents have done. I know that there is wisdom in youth. As a baby, my first words were: 'Seize the means of production.'

If anything, people become more retarded as they grow older. The most intelligent person in the world at present is the teenager Greta Thunberg (Peace Be Upon Her). And by far the stupidest is that 'Professor' Jordan Peterson. I haven't read any of his books, but apparently he's some kind of shadowy beef-munching Mephistopheles figure who thinks that lobsters should tidy their rooms or something.

I am fully aware that the word 'retarded' has become an offensive pejorative term, but I am reclaiming it. This is because to be 'retarded' simply means 'to move backwards'. And as paradoxical as it may seem, in order to progress we *must* move backwards to a time before our culture became infected with democracy, free speech and facts. I feel no compunction, therefore, in declaring that social justice is a profound form of retardation.

As a young person in a world swarming with crypto-fascists, you will need guidance from one whose benevolence is beyond doubt. Enter Titania McGrath.

That's me, by the way.

Your parents are not to be trusted. At least one of them is likely to be straight, which is an aberration that has plagued humankind since the aeon of the velociraptors. Given that sexuality is fluid, the World Health Organization really should classify heterosexual desire as a severe mental and behavioural disorder. Believe me, future generations will thank us if we successfully eliminate heterosexuality.

Many of you will have been gestated in a traditional female womb, and been arbitrarily assigned a sex at birth. You will have been told you are a 'girl' or, even worse, a 'boy'. You will have attended an indoctrination camp known as a 'school' and will have been programmed by the media to believe ludicrous lies. This book is your first step towards undoing that damage.

To the little girls who are reading this, it is important that you learn that you will always be oppressed, no matter how much you try to distract yourselves with weekend breaks in the Loire Valley or the occasional spree at Harrods. As for the boys, you really should transition to female as soon as possible so that you might begin to understand the extent of our persecution.

Let me put this as clearly as possible. Your teachers hate you. Your parents hate you. And as for your grandparents, they're just gnarled and embittered gnomes whose only redeeming feature is that they won't be around for much longer.

As this is the first time I have written anything aimed at young children, I have undertaken a great deal of research on how best to go about it. I have been reliably informed that kids adore illustrations because they help to clarify the meaning of the text. With that in mind, here is a diagram which will help you to better understand the complexities of intersectional activism.

Intersectional Activism: How It Works

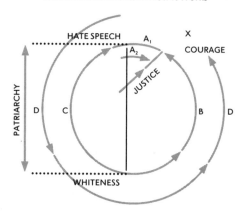

X = VIRTUE   A = DIVERSITY   B = HETERONORMATIVITY
C = OPPRESSION   D = LIVED EXPERIENCE

I think we can learn a lot from this.

So let me tell you a bit about myself. I am Titania McGrath: scourge of the patriarchy, breaker of chains, the embodiment of social justice. If truth bombs were eggs, I'd be a chicken. So if you're unsure about which opinions to have, this is the book for you.

In addition to being a feminist and a socialist, I'm also the most important poet of my generation. To prove it, a selection of my best work is included in this volume. My speciality is the genre known as 'slam'. So when you read the poems, imagine that I'm reciting them in a vaguely urban accent. Take great care when approaching my poetry, as it tends to expose new layers of meaning with every reading, like the very wokest of onions.

I have started performing my more shocking and evocative poems at environmental protests, such as the ever-popular 'Mother Earth is Not Your Slut'. I tend to recite it completely naked, except for a pashmina fashioned from interlaced earthworms. Some people find my performance so moving that they actually have to leave.

In addition to my lyrical prowess, I am also an oppressed minority. I'm ecosexual, which means I only have sex with plants and vegetables. I'm trans-disabled, which means that I am permitted to use the more spacious public toilet facilities in spite of my functioning legs. And I'm also hay-racial, which means that my ethnic identity tends to fluctuate depending on the pollen count.

I have a reputation not only for my intelligence, but also for my righteous anger. Like Joan of Arc, I have successfully fought for justice against incredible odds. But unlike Joan of Arc, I haven't made the dumb mistake of getting myself burned to death in the process.

I didn't ask to be an icon, but part of growing up is to accept the role that fate decrees. You will learn this as you reach adulthood. Obviously, your role is unlikely to be as important as mine. You'll probably end up working in a supermarket or something. But even a lowly shop assistant can be woke.

People often ask me to define 'woke'. I don't need to. I am the living definition of the word. But if you're interested to know more, you should tell your parents to buy a copy of my first book, *Woke: A Guide to Social Justice*, which has a particularly strong chapter on how to defeat capitalism. It's available on Amazon.

And now, in spite of the patriarchal forces that would see me vanquished, I have penned *My First Little Book of Intersectional Activism*. There have been many progressive children's books flooding the market of late, such as *Feminist Baby*, *C is for Consent* and *The Little Girl Who Gave Zero Fucks*. Perhaps the most accomplished is *Good Night Stories for Rebel Girls*, which pays tribute to feminist role models such as Michelle Obama, Maya Angelou and Yoko Ono. My favourite chapter is the one on Coco Chanel, the most empowering of all the Nazi collaborators.

Needless to say, my book is even better. In a series of groundbreaking and poignant chapters, I shall take you on a journey with the most inspiring individuals in history, such as Emmeline Pankhurst, Hillary Clinton and Joseph Stalin. Even if you haven't yet learned how to read, you should carry it with you wherever you go to prove that you're not a bigot.

Some of you might be thinking that, in the wake of a deadly pandemic, social justice activism should take a back seat, or that our concerns now seem relatively trivial. On the contrary, voices such as mine have never been more urgently needed. It is crucial that we all work together to ensure that this pandemic does not distract us from the far more serious problem of people being misgendered on Twitter.

Besides, too often we are quick to judge and demonise those we do not understand. As a vegan and humanitarian, I welcome refugees of any species. And yes, that includes the coronavirus.

It is surely no coincidence that the so-called 'medical community' has decided to focus its ire on a Chinese virus rather than, say, German Measles, Japanese Encephalitis or Rocky Mountain Spotted Fever. I consider the search for a vaccine to be profoundly racist.

Already, the virus has been renamed 'COVID-19' in a flagrant attempt at dehumanisation. Do you know who else was given numbers instead of names? That's right. Those two gay robots in *Star Wars*.

Another problem we now face is that bigots like that oxidised hobgoblin Donald Trump are routinely using the phrase 'Chinese virus' as a racist dog whistle. On the other hand, it should go without saying that denying the coronavirus its right to a national identity post-migration is also a racist dog whistle. Therefore, those of us who oppose racism must be sure that we never refer to the virus as Chinese, or deny that it is, in fact, Chinese.

So already we can see how intersectional activism is more relevant than ever in these strange times. If the apocalypse does come, we need to ensure that it doesn't disproportionately affect minority groups.

In a sense, we should be grateful for the coronavirus, because my period of self-isolation afforded me the time and the opportunity to write this book. Given the importance of my work, the global dissemination of a lethal virus seems a small price to pay.

It has been a gratifying experience to write about all my favourite role models. Some are historical. Others are still alive today and actively working to educate the masses in the correct way to think. Even the Royal Family has achieved a heightened state of wokeness thanks to the influence of Meghan Markle, to whom I have dedicated a chapter of this book. In many ways, Meghan is the archetypal modern feminist. She is young, photogenic, internet savvy, and is known to perform creative feats with an avocado.

I've had to leave out some of the more obvious luminaries, like Florence Nightingale. But given that Nightingale never said anything in support of non-binary rights, we must assume that she was transphobic. As for Rosa Parks, I think she gets too much publicity as it is and, to be honest, it sometimes feels as though she's stealing my thunder. I'm a little tired of being described as the 'modern-day Rosa Parks'. For one thing, I wouldn't be seen dead on public transport.

The same goes for Jesus Christ (to whom I am often compared) who they killed just because he was a Palestinian. As a staunch anti-capitalist, I've always been inspired by the story of Jesus attacking the moneylenders in the temple. I did a similar thing when I was four years old in my local branch of HSBC. Believe me, it took them several minutes to pick up all those pens from the floor.

Another great figure from history who didn't make the cut was Dr Martin Luther King, because I feel that his message has now been superseded by my own. Because actually, it is *I* who have a dream.

I have a dream that little children will one day live in a nation where they will be judged not by the content of their character, but by the colour of their skin, in order to fulfil diversity quotas and deconstruct the inherent toxicity of whiteness.

I have a dream that little black boys and little black girls and little black gender-nonconforming children will be able to work as one to dismantle oppressive institutionalised power structures and cis-dominant heteronormative discourses of privilege.

And in these pages, my dream shall come true.

ALYSSA MILANO

Once upon a time there was an actor called Alyssa whose genre-defining performances had earned her national-treasure status, particularly in *Who's the Boss?*, *My Name is Earl*, *Charmed*, and the immortal *Beverly Hills Chihuahua 2*.

But it was her unceasing campaigning for social justice which made her closer akin to a deity than a human being. For she was not merely Alyssa; she was the embodiment of all humanity. As she herself proclaimed: 'I'm trans. I'm a person of colour. I'm an immigrant. I'm a lesbian. I'm a gay man. I'm the disabled. I'm everything.'

In this, she was probably channelling Mahatma Gandhi who, when asked if he were a Hindu, famously replied: 'Yes, I am. I am also a Christian, a Muslim, a Buddhist and a Jew.' (He hated Sikhs.)

It was Alyssa's unique combination of selflessness and modesty that marked her out for greatness. She was largely ignored, which only goes to show the extent of her historical significance. She was a new Cassandra, screaming truth into the deaf ears of peoplekind.

I think we're in the time when the metaphysical world is so interesting.

ALYSSA MILANO

Her activism knew no bounds. She once wore a dress made entirely of vegetables in order to show solidarity with the vegan community. Even her pet cat was a proud vegan. It did keep chasing birds in the garden, but it probably just assumed they were some kind of flying vegetable.

Alyssa was one of the first to make the connection between Trump voters and the Ku Klux Klan by observing that: 'The red MAGA hat is the new white hood.' Her point was conclusively proven when a fifteen-year-old boy wearing a MAGA hat was slapped by a man at a polling site in New Hampshire. What more evidence do you need that Trump supporters incite violence?

Like all important activists, most of Alyssa's work took place on Twitter. 'Be super careful,' she once tweeted. 'Sex is extremely dangerous for women. No matter who it's with.' She urged us to mistrust all men and their essentially toxic masculinity. I have taken this to be a guiding principle in my life. When a male stranger approached me recently to ask for directions, I pepper-sprayed him in the face. You can't be too careful.

As an activist at the forefront of the #MeToo movement, Alyssa knew that there are only two kinds of men: rapists and rapists-in-waiting. Any male who has ever thought about a woman in a remotely sexual way is a predator, and any man who has had sexual dreams about women is guilty of dream-rape and should turn himself over to the police.

Alyssa was a firm advocate of the #MeToo movement's 'believe women' mantra, except when the Democratic party's nominee for president, Joe Biden, was accused of sexual assault. In this case it was perfectly clear to Alyssa that Biden had only been sniffing women's hair in order to ensure that they weren't scented in such a way as to entice sexual predators like Donald Trump.

She was a vocal advocate of 'Equal Pay Day', which raises awareness of the gender pay gap. Even in 2020, some women are *still* paid less money simply for choosing lower-paid jobs or working fewer hours. It's an absolute scandal.

To give a specific example, firefighters in the United States (96 per cent male) earn an average salary of $46,870 per year, whereas receptionists (95 per cent female) earn roughly $35,920. The gender pay gap is *not* a myth.

Thankfully, we have seen some pushback in recent years. In Melbourne, Australia, a vegan café took matters into its own hands and began charging an 18 per cent 'man tax' and offering priority seating to its female customers. For some reason, it lost money and had to close down. Only in an oppressive patriarchy like ours would charging men more for the same services turn out to be an unsuccessful business model.

But it was Alyssa's proposed 'sex strike' to protest against new abortion laws that really established her as the most radical activist of her generation. 'Our reproductive rights are being erased,' she posted on Twitter. 'Until women have legal control over our own bodies we just cannot risk pregnancy. JOIN ME by not having sex until we get bodily autonomy back. I'm calling for a #SexStrike. Pass it on.'

As women, it is our duty to stand up for our right to an abortion by ensuring that none of us gets pregnant.

GRETA THUNBERG

Once upon a time there was a girl called Greta who came from Sweden, which is that place in northern Europe with all the extra vowels. She cared passionately about climate change, and because she was young and suffered from Asperger's Syndrome it meant that anyone who questioned any of her ideas could simply be dismissed as a nasty old bully.

Greta was the most important prophet the world had ever seen, even more so than John the Baptist or David Icke. Whenever she spoke at major political institutions, berating the older generation for condemning their offspring to certain death, the effect was mesmerising. She truly touched the heartstrings of everyone she shouted at.

She had supernatural powers, and was able to levitate from country to country without the need for conventional transportation powered by scarce fossil fuels. She could speak the language of trees, and was able to heal damaged badgers using just her tongue.

It's not about Meatloaf.

GRETA THUNBERG

Cripples and lepers would often reach out to touch the hem of her organic yellow raincoat as she walked by, in the hope of being healed. After she was declared *Time* magazine's 'Person of the Year', there were multiple worldwide reports of the missing limbs of amputees instantaneously growing back.

One of Greta's favourite pastimes was to point out that the world's elders had completely sold out Generation Z. As such, she inspired swathes of children to selflessly play truant from school and organise their own protests. Since when have activists required an education?

Oftentimes you would see infants of no more than six years of age holding placards bearing slogans such as 'Regeneration Not Deforestation'. It's so moving when children spontaneously come out with the things we've taught them to say.

Greta's influence extended to the political sphere. Government officials from around the world would beg to attend her speeches in order to be better educated by her intuitive wisdom. Before long, young politicians were taking the fight to the wizened old males of yesteryear who had so devastated the planet. Chlöe Swarbrick, a millennial Green Party MP in New Zealand's parliament, made international headlines when she lambasted her ageing colleagues, Greta-style, for their complicity in the environmental catastrophe. When challenged, Swarbrick simply retorted: 'OK, boomer.' Why bother arguing when you have an empowering meme like that up your sleeve?

To be honest, I didn't even know New Zealand had its own parliament. I thought it was just a timeshare for rich Australians.

Greta's tireless work roused a fresh generation of eco-warriors, who would often congregate in the central areas of London. This was extremely convenient because very few of the protestors lived beyond Zone Three. On any given day, thousands of Greta's disciples would gather in tents while bearded men in red togas chanted paeans to Pan and the woodland nymphs.

As well as being important, these events were a great deal of fun. There was radical street theatre, acoustic lesbian quintets, and angry teenagers reciting haiku about why we need more manatees. Some activists would glue their babies to the doors of petrol stations. The babies would invariably start crying, which just proves how worried they were about the future of the planet.

Inevitably, there was a backlash among some of the more reactionary elements of the media. Many criticised Greta's supporters for being overwhelmingly white and middle class, but this was simply not true. Occasionally there were families who brought along their Filipino au pairs.

If you are interested in an insightful and unbiased analysis of Greta Thunberg's powers, I would highly recommend the documentary by *Vice* magazine: *Make the World Greta Again*. For those who don't know, *Vice* is at the very forefront of searing investigative journalism. We can still feel the seismic reverberations generated by articles such as 'Beards Aren't Cool Anymore', 'What's the Best Kind of Gun to Conceal Inside Your Ladyparts?', 'Gluten-Free People are Getting Laid Way More Than the Rest of Us', and the classic 'I Ate Myself Out Using My iPhone and It Was Pretty Good'.

ROBIN DIANGELO

SOCIOLOGIST

Once upon a time there was a woman called Robin who became a prominent academic and developed a concept known as 'white fragility'. It was a brilliant theory that immediately explained the bizarre phenomenon of why some white people don't like being called racist if they've never said or done anything racist.

Robin pioneered what became known as 'Whiteness Studies'. She argued that treating people the same irrespective of the colour of their skin was 'dangerous', because it failed to take into account the oppressive power structures which are embedded in society. In other words, there is nothing more racist than when white people insist on treating black people as equals.

As Robin explained in an article for the *Guardian*: 'White people assume niceness is the answer to racial inequality. It's not.' In order to combat racism, therefore, we all need to stop being nice to people of colour.

In any case, race is a social construct. And it is surely no coincidence that it is only ever privileged white

It is inevitable that you are racist.

ROBIN DIANGELO

people who dispute this. If you look at a white person's DNA under a microscope, you won't see a helix. It'll be in the shape of a swastika.

Robin toiled unflaggingly to raise awareness of white privilege and the advantages it provides. For instance, a white man can walk into any pet shop, pick out one of their finest Pomeranians, and the salesperson isn't going to call the police assuming he's buying it for the purposes of ritualistic voodoo sacrifice. That's the kind of staggering privilege we're talking about here.

Although critics pointed out the inconsistencies and errors in her logic, Robin was careful to explain it all through the language of intersectionality and critical race theory. This meant that very few people understood what she was going on about anyway.

Robin's courageous work inspired a whole new generation of anti-racist activists, including myself. After reading her book *White Fragility*, I developed an action plan of what we could do to combat inequality. Here are my main suggestions:

- All white people should be taxed an extra 40 per cent on their wages to provide reparations to people of colour.

- White couples should be forced to apply for a licence to reproduce. And even if successful, there should be a one-baby limit. (This one-baby system has been tried and tested and it *works*. When they implemented it in China hardly any white babies were born at all.)

- Given the horribly disproportionate number of black and Hispanic convicts in the US, we need to urge all white people to take up mugging so that we can develop a more representative prison population.

But Robin's influence didn't end with *White Fragility*. Her theory that whiteness is about much more than skin colour soon became a mainstream view. In October 2019, two Indian teenagers were arrested at a football game in New Jersey after harassing and urinating on a group of black school-girls. An article in the *New York Times* explained that although the perpetrators were not themselves white, they were 'enacting whiteness' through their attack.

This was one of the fundamental points that Robin's fearless research has demonstrated: only white people can be racist. She preferred to describe discrimination within ethnic groups as 'colourism'. So, for instance:

> **A HOMELESS WHITE MAN CLAIMING NOT TO BE PRIVILEGED**
>
> **= RACISM**
>
> **THE SUDANESE GOVERNMENT'S MASSACRE OF NON-ARABS**
>
> **= COLOURISM**

To put it another way, if Oprah Winfrey were to spit at Debbie Gibson, that wouldn't be racist, because whites have all the power. In fact, Gibson would have to apologise.

I would take this a step further. Since it is impossible for black people to be racist, any white person who is not being racist is committing behavioural blackface. Therefore, all non-racist white people are racist.

Ultimately, Robin's work reminds us that humanity will only thrive if it is divided strictly into racial groups and treated differently. We will never defeat the plague of racism until people of colour have their own spaces away from whites. I suggest we start with schools, restaurants and drinking fountains.

ABRAHAM LINCOLN

PRESIDENT

Once upon a time there was a president called Abraham. Very few people know that Abraham was trans, but I have decided that she was.

This is known as 'retrospective transitioning', whereby you can choose an individual from history and assign them a new identity in order to make them more representative of minority groups. I'm thinking of writing a book about how the Ancient Greek philosophers were actually a group of black lesbian vegan insurrectionists.

The great thing about deciding that Abraham was trans is that we can now say in all honesty that there has been at least one female president of the United States of America. This is particularly important ever since Hillary Clinton was robbed of the presidency on the very flimsy grounds that she failed to get enough votes.

Abraham was a glimmer of joy in the country's otherwise dismal political history, which was merely a succession of straight white males fucking everything

Make
America
woke again.
ABRAHAM LINCOLN

up. There was only ever one black president, Barack Obama, but his mother was white which made him 50 per cent problematic.

Before turning to politics, Abraham worked in the legal profession. She was awarded her law licence in 1839, a full thirty-three years before Arabella Mansfield, the fraud who is typically credited with being the US's first female lawyer. It's essential that trans women reclaim their historical precedence over cisgender scum like Arabella.

Abraham was most famous for her indefatigable efforts to abolish slavery, although she was only partly successful. Due to institutionalised power structures, black people in America today are more oppressed than any of their ancestors ever were and must be treated as victims at all times. Even the ones who are millionaires.

Nowadays it is up to us to finish the work that Abraham begun. We all need to play our part in making reparations. So whenever you encounter a black person, give them some loose change to show that you care.

And remember, as white liberals it is our duty to protect people of colour, to safeguard their dignity by speaking on their behalf.

Without us, they are nothing.

ABŪ BAKR AL-BAGHDADI

AUSTERE RELIGIOUS SCHOLAR

Once upon a time there was an Iraqi man called Abū. Lots of people referred to him as a 'terrorist', but we know that he was actually an austere religious scholar because that's how the *Washington Post* described him when he died. It was only the conservative media who tried to smear him as a 'mass murderer'.

Abū was the leader of a group of austere religious scholars known collectively as 'ISIS'. Many people were frightened of them because austere religious scholarly 'terrorism' was apparently on the rise. It was impossible to determine why such tragedies were occurring. Let's take the attack on London Bridge in June 2017, where three austere religious scholars drove into pedestrians before going on a rampage, stabbing people at will while shouting: 'This is for Allah.' The sad truth is that their motives are for ever likely to remain a mystery.

The media never had anything nice to say about Abū, which just proved how resentful they were that

Oh fuck, they've brought a dog.

ABŪ BAKR AL-BAGHDADI

a person of colour had been successful in his chosen career. Others put this down to Islamophobia. It could hardly be a coincidence that the press were always reporting on Islamist suicide bombers, while Catholic suicide bombers never seemed to get any attention at all.

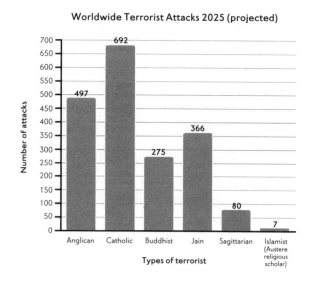

Worldwide Terrorist Attacks 2025 (projected)

(Source: Titania McGrath)

We saw proof of this media bias with the demonisa-tion of Shamima Begum, a teenager who was forced to flee London to join ISIS because Muslims were under-represented on the BBC. When her husband had finished beheading everyone, she naturally got bored and tried to return to the UK, but the Islamophobic government refused. They argued that she had surrendered her right to return when she joined a genocidal, medieval death-cult. But surely we have to recognise that teenagers make mistakes. My sister got caught stealing a croissant during her gap year in Marseille, and we let her back in.

As an adherent of the Religion of Peace™ and one of the world's leading austere religious scholars, Abū believed in acts of peaceful genocide and austere executions, as well as keeping sex slaves in an austere and peaceful way.

Eventually he was assassinated by the US government, which has rightly been described as a 'terrorist regime' by oppressed millionaire actor Rose McGowan. An army dog was awarded a medal of bravery for his role in the operation, which just goes to show that even American dogs are Islamophobic.

MEGHAN MARKLE

O nce upon a time there was an American girl called Meghan whose destiny it was to single-handedly reinvent the British Royal Family. Let me tell you how she did it.

One day in 2016, Meghan went on a blind date with a boy called Harry Windsor, grandson of Queen Elizabeth II and sixth in line to the British throne. Prince Harry often went on blind dates, as this is the traditional method of courtship for ginger-haired men.

Almost instantly Meghan saw her opportunity. She understood that the Royal Family was an archaic institution in desperate need of reform. And so she hatched a scheme to transform the monarchy from within, and her first step was to marry the pasty-faced redhead that nobody else wanted.

Harry was excited to be marrying a big TV star like Meghan, even though he couldn't actually name any of the shows she'd starred in. At the time he was a dissolute young rake who drank too much, partied

On my face, I use Creme De La Mer
The Eye Balm Intense and Tatcha
Deep Brightening Serum.

MEGHAN MARKLE

too hard, and was even once photographed wearing a Nazi swastika. But at least he had the good grace to lie about it and pretend he'd been going to a fancy-dress party.

On their second date, Meghan and Harry decided it would be mutually beneficial to fall in love and so announced on Instagram that they were getting married. Many commentators in the media applauded the fact that the Royal Family was finally poised to embrace diversity. Up until now, this stale old institution had been staunchly British (except for Prince Philip who was Greek, and the rest of them who were German).

Meghan's influence on Harry was immediately apparent. The first thing she did after their wedding was to decolonise his wardrobe. This meant throwing out anything made by companies who had exploited workers in the Third World, anything which appropriated fabrics or designs from other cultures, and anything with a swastika on it. This is why Harry spent the first few days of his honeymoon sitting around in just his pants.

It took Meghan less than three months to transform Harry into a woke icon for the Instagram generation. He took up yoga, meditation, and Wiccan embroidery, and at the same time gave up alcohol, cigarettes, caffeine and all other known forms of joy.

Then one day Meghan discovered that she was pregnant. Everyone in the country was tremendously excited about the prospect of a mixed-race royal baby, but Prince Archie turned out to be disappointingly pale. (I go darker than that after a weekend in Val d'Isère, for fuck's sake.)

One day, *British Vogue* invited Meghan to be guest editor. She accepted enthusiastically, because there's no better way to promote equality and expose the evils of consumer culture than by fronting one of the world's leading fashion magazines.

Meghan helped Harry to write an article about 'unconscious bias', which is basically when a person imbibes the pernicious views of society without even being aware of it. As Harry repeatedly insisted, he was a freethinker who would never allow those around him to control his opinions. This was one of the very first things that Meghan taught him to say.

In spite of all their efforts to save the world, the press were always picking on poor Meghan and Harry, so they eventually decided to stand down as 'senior royals'. This was an excellent decision, because it meant that although they would continue to receive attention from the press, they wouldn't have to bother doing any actual work.

To celebrate, Meghan immediately chartered a private jet to Switzerland in order to attend another conference on climate change. Harry gave one of his famous barefoot speeches, which symbolised his deep connection to the earth. It was also practical, because Meghan had thrown most of his shoes away after she found out they weren't vegan.

And they both lived happily ever after.

INTERLUDE: HOW TO WIN AN ARGUMENT

Debate is a form of violence. If you have joined the debating club at your school, you are essentially a terrorist.

If I ever have one slight point of political disagreement with somebody, that's enough for me to know that they're a Nazi. Some of these people claim to be 'conservatives', but I refuse to believe that anyone could sincerely hold conservative opinions. It's far more likely that they're just mouthpieces funded clandestinely by foreign powers.

Nevertheless, sometimes arguments are inevitable. I often find that my opponents will try to blindside me with 'facts' and 'logic', slippery manoeuvres that end up making it look as though I don't know what I'm talking about.

But through practice and perseverance I have learned how best to deal with such cretins. One particularly effective technique is to use their own 'logical' tactics against them. Consider the following syllogism, for instance:

- **BESTIALITY IS A CRIMINAL OFFENCE.**

- **MEN ARE NO BETTER THAN ANIMALS.**

- **ERGO, SEX WITH MEN SHOULD BE ILLEGAL.**

Let's try a more specific example. When various Conservative politicians in the UK were running for the leadership of the party in 2019, the *Independent* ran an article which complained that the contest was 'dominated by white men'. One of the candidates, Sajid Javid, objected on the grounds that his parents were Pakistani immigrants. Using a process of logic, we can dismiss his argument, thus:

- **SAJID JAVID HAS JUDGED HIMSELF TO BE NON-WHITE SOLELY ON THE BASIS OF HIS SKIN COLOUR.**

- **ANY JUDGEMENT BASED ON SKIN COLOUR IS RACIST.**

- **ONLY WHITE PEOPLE CAN BE RACIST.**

- **THEREFORE, SAJID JAVID IS WHITE.**

Checkmate, you Tory maggot.

There are many other foolproof techniques which you might think about adopting if you are cornered into a debate. Firstly, one needs to consider carefully one's choice of words. 'Fascist' and 'Nazi' are excellent examples of terms which never fail to undermine the confidence of the unwoke. I routinely use them to describe anyone who voted for Brexit, and the fact that people act so defensively when you compare them to Hitler only goes to show that the analogy is sound.

'Bigot' is another useful word. It is defined as 'a person who is intolerant towards those holding different opinions', so I tend to use it against anyone who has the audacity to disagree with me.

Secondly, you should explicitly and vocally assess your opponent on the basis of their privilege. If, for instance, they are a straight white male, their opinion is bound to be wrong. A transblack translesbian, on the

STRAIGHT WHITE MALE
= BAD

TRANSBLACK TRANSLESBIAN
= GOOD

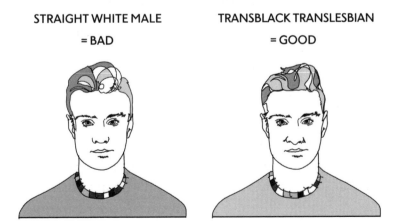

other hand, is part of an oppressed group and is therefore almost always correct about absolutely everything.

The other sure-fire strategy is to diagnose one's opponents with a 'phobia', defined as 'an extreme or irrational fear'. Needless to say, it isn't possible to debate an irrational person. So when I decide that someone is homophobic, biphobic, transphobic, queerphobic, whorephobic, fatphobic, Islamophobic, xenophobic or vegaphobic, this means that I am not obliged to debate them.

One of my other methods is to explain my perspective using the language of intersectional feminist theory. For instance, instead of saying: 'Straight white men are evil,' you could simply say: 'Y'all need to stop mainstreaming the normalisation of hetero-pestilential androcentric hegemony through the commodification of blackness in proxi-fascist opposition to the sociopolitically marginalised'. The unreconstructed bigots of the right are rarely well schooled in such terminology, and at this point will usually just give up.

In this, I have been inspired by the bold work of Foucauldian queer theorists such as Judith Butler, Gayle Rubin and Eve Kosofsky Sedgwick. I have fond memories of protesting against the gender-normative

implications of my Home Economics class at primary
school by stitching my favourite quotation from
Sedgwick onto a pillowcase. It simply read: 'In conso-
nance with my emphasis on the performative relations
of double and conflicted definition, the theorised
prescription for a practical politics implicit in these
readings is for a multi-pronged movement whose
idealist and materialist impulses, whose minority-
model and universalist-model strategies, and for that
matter whose gender-separatist and gender-integrative
analyses would likewise proceed in parallel without
any high premium placed on ideological rationaliza-
tion between them.' This is activist prose at its most
eloquent and powerful.

But perhaps the best way to win an argument is
simply to refuse to talk to your opponent in the first
place. Why should those with the wrong opinions be
free to express themselves? The very concept of 'free
speech' is a racist dog whistle. When I've made this
point in the past, I've been accused of living in an
'echo chamber'. But I've asked all my close friends
and they agree that this is definitely not the case.

In addition, the phrase 'racist dog whistle' is itself a
racist dog whistle. As journalist Ben Faulding has
argued: 'Dogs are a tool of white supremacy and
gentrification ... There is research that shows how

white newcomers dogwalking routes stake out territory. And white owners use their pets to socialise with other white owners excluding minorities.' Likewise, gerbils are a tool of anti-Semitism because they can be trained to nibble on the sidelocks of orthodox Jews.

So next time you're confronted with a right-wing reactionary who is keen to bully you with their thoughts, try some of the strategies I've outlined here. Brand them a 'Nazi', bludgeon them with intersectional jargon or, better still, pretend they don't exist.

JACK DORSEY

ENTREPRENEUR

Once upon a time there was a man called Jack who had invented a way for social justice activists to deliver their message of truth to the fallen. It was called 'Twitter', a forum via which love, tolerance and intersectionality could be spread across the globe with the aid of a few hashtags.

Jack was a very spiritual man who spent much of his time on Vipassana retreats on small islands in the Indian Ocean that he had bought from the local savages at a very reasonable price. And it was on these retreats, through a strict regime of Vedic meditation, that he was able to achieve a state of total mindlessness. Twitter was born.

Jack liked to wear T-shirts with '#StayWoke' printed on them to prove to everyone that he was a good person. But this was more than just a slogan for Jack. He lived and breathed that hashtag. He knew that the most effective way to achieve his socialist utopia was to earn as much money as possible. As a billionaire CEO of a major international corporation he was

I was fascinated with jeans, because you can impress your life upon the jeans you wear. The way you sit imprints on the jeans.

JACK DORSEY

uniquely qualified to understand what was best for ordinary working folk, which is why he made sure that Twitter censored all material that might hurt the poor plebeians or influence them to do bad things.

He started by deleting the accounts of nasty right-wing people like Alex Jones, host of American website *InfoWars*. Jones had been spreading fake news and wild conspiracy theories, unlike all the responsible left-wing journalists who had done so much to teach us about how the Russian government had tricked everyone into voting for Donald Trump.

Censorship is the key to freedom. To this end, Jack created the 'Trust and Safety Council', a group of like-minded overlords who would monitor the content of Twitter's users and filter out all problematic material. This proved to be a great success, enabling woke warriors like myself to roar our eternal truths across the digital savannah of cyberspace without fear of contradiction.

Inevitably, Jack sometimes made mistakes. In September 2018, I was subjected to a 'permanent suspension' (a semantic contradiction, but let's not quibble) for tweeting that I was planning to attend a UKIP rally in order to punch people in the name of tolerance. The decision was eventually reversed due to an outcry from my disciples. In a sense, I was grateful for the time off. I took the opportunity to visit my gîte near Buis-les-Baronnies, where I could relax and contemplate my oppression.

So do not listen when parents and teachers tell you that too much time on your smartphones can be damaging to your mental health. It is only through social media that we can realign the world in accordance with woke values. It also means we don't have to actually talk to anyone face to face, which is convenient because most people are fairly unattractive. It also solves the problem of having to decipher regional accents which, let's be honest, are incomprehensible at the best of times.

Oh, and if you're going to be a social justice activist on Twitter, always make sure that you announce your pronouns in your bio. That way, when you're calling your opponents evil lowlife scumbags, trying to get them fired, or gloating if they die, everyone will know that you're actually incredibly compassionate.

EMMELINE PANKHURST

SUFFRAGETTE

Once upon a time there was a feminist called Emmeline who lived in a country called England in which women were not allowed to vote. Well, Emmeline wasn't having any of that, and so she led a group of women to fight for equal rights under the banner of the 'suffragettes'.

Emmeline wasn't the perfect feminist. For one thing, she had taken her husband's surname, which would suggest an unhealthy degree of internalised misogyny. Let's face it, women who relinquish their birth name may as well have 'property of the patriarchy' branded on their tits.

All married women are slaves. All married men are slaveowners. And bridesmaids are essentially SS guards in taffeta.

The journey to women's equality had been long and arduous. As Sally Hines, Professor of Sociology and Gender Identities at the University of Leeds, once observed: 'Before the Enlightenment the female skeleton didn't exist.' Up until that point, women had to crawl around like slugs.

I'm fucking sick of this massive skirt.
Look at it. I look like a twat.

EMMELINE PANKHURST

But it was Emmeline who taught us how to fly, and we haven't stopped flying since. In 2018, one hundred years after votes were finally granted to women, the magazine *British Vogue* published a piece about 'The New Suffragettes', which featured a group of modern-day feminists who were continuing Emmeline's legacy by blogging, writing provocative tweets, and generally becoming rich and famous.

They included the politician Stella Creasy (who likes to celebrate female empowerment by reminding everyone how oppressed we are), Reni Eddo-Lodge (the journalist who wrote a book urging us not to talk to white people in an effort to promote racial harmony) and Dina Torkia (the hijab-wearing social-media sensation who has shown how it's possible to be both sexy and independent without exposing your hair like some kind of shameful whore).

Another member of the 'New Suffragettes', the artist Gillian Wearing, noted that their struggle was even 'harder than fighting for the vote'. Indeed, compared to the oppression that women in the UK face today, the likes of Emmeline had it easy.

That is not to say we should not be grateful for Emmeline's work, but nor should we be complacent about what has yet to be achieved. Women are by far the most persecuted of all the minorities, possibly because there are so many of us. Some anthropologists estimate that approximately 50 per cent of the population is female. When it comes to minorities, that's quite a lot.

So let's hear it for Emmeline, one of the first women to realise that masculinity is not only toxic but as fragile as a butterfly's hymen. As the esteemed scholar and philosopher Laurie Penny has said: 'Toxic masculinity is killing the world.' Feminism, then, is not simply a matter of ensuring emancipation from the shackles of the patriarchy, but is nothing less than the prevention of Armageddon.

JUSSIE SMOLLETT

MARTYR

O nce upon a time, there was an actor called Jussie who was the victim of a terrible hate crime on account of the fact that he was black and gay. He had been out in the early hours of the morning in the city of Chicago, innocently browsing for sandwiches, when two white men in ski masks ambushed him, wrapped a noose around his neck, doused him with chemicals, and chanted: 'This is MAGA country.' And although many have since claimed that this didn't actually happen, most sensible people agree that exposing the homophobia and racism of Trump's America is far more important than the 'truth'.

In any case, only a racist homophobe would deny Jussie's lived experience. The lies about him were unforgivable. The police insisted that the white assailants were actually two Nigerian men that Jussie had hired after meeting them at his gym. Even if this were the case, for this act alone Jussie ought to be congratulated. By offering jobs to two unemployed black

56

The Mighty Ducks was a great experience, and I don't shy away from that.

JUSSIE SMOLLETT

actors, he would have already done far more than most casting directors.

Besides, to describe the attack as 'fake' is a racist microaggression. We're talking about actors here. I've never heard anyone in the media describe Robert de Niro, Tim Curry or Meryl Streep as *fakes*. It seems quite apparent that they hold white people to different standards.

Jussie's terrible ordeal reminds us that there is no such thing as a 'fake victim'. Reality is subjective. If Jussie decides that he is a victim, then he is a victim. Anyway, what the hell was he meant to do? Just hang around and *hope* he got attacked? The real world doesn't work like that.

In the controversy that followed, the producers of the hit TV show *Empire* decided to remove Jussie's character from the final two episodes of the season. They actually felt emboldened to erase a gay black man from their show. This is exactly the kind of behaviour that proves that Jussie would have been perfectly within his rights to raise awareness by staging an attack in the first place. Which he didn't do, because it *definitely* happened.

Anyone who has ever claimed that Jussie Smollett is a fraud must now be prosecuted. Lying about hate crime can never be permitted in a civilised society.

MARY WHITEHOUSE

Once upon a time, there was a woman called Mary who was very upset about all the nasty television programmes and films that people were watching. As an early pioneer of the social justice movement, she understood more than anyone that whatever happens on TV ends up being copied by working-class people who don't understand how fiction works.

Poor people are like lemmings; they don't know what's best for them, they follow each other blindly, and they sometimes live in tunnels. So in the 1960s, Mary set up a 'Clean Up TV' campaign that would put a stop to those programmes which were leading the proletariat astray. Then, in the 1980s, she was a major force in the crusade against 'video nasties' which led to a number of films being banned. One of these was the horror movie *Driller Killer*, which perpetuated the obsolete stereotype that only men are able to use power tools.

A similar campaign could work today, and would target mainstream films that promote hatred. To give

AIDS is a judgment we have brought upon ourselves.

MARY WHITEHOUSE

a recent example, the movie *It* – in which Bill Skarsgård plays a killer clown – normalises the idea that those who use gender-neutral pronouns tend to be psychopaths who wear too much make-up.

Mary's legacy lives on in a new generation of woke activists, many of whom work in prominent areas of the media, the arts, the law, education and government. Even the publishing industry has started hiring 'sensitivity readers' to vet their authors' work and excise any potentially offensive material. So, for instance, if a white male author were to write about a black woman, a sensitivity reader would point out that he lacks the necessary lived experience to do so and would remove the character forthwith; a great victory for inclusivity.

Mary's ongoing influence was also felt when the Advertising Standards Authority in the UK banned two ads with problematic portrayals of men and women. The first was for Volkswagen's electric e-Golf vehicle, which clearly showed a woman next to a pram and therefore dangerously implied that some women can be mothers.

The second was for Philadelphia cream cheese, which depicted two new fathers leaving their babies on a conveyor belt while they were busy stuffing their faces with cheesy snacks. Although it is true that males are irresponsible and gluttonous, it is genuinely offensive to see white people eating off conveyor belts. Only the Japanese are allowed to do that.

Those who claim that advertisements exist in order to sell products are missing the point. Adverts are there to educate the masses about social justice. This is why the high street chain Boots recently launched its empowering 'Let's Feel Good About Summer' campaign, which emphasised that you don't need to be physically attractive to wear a swimsuit. Gillette went a step further, making a brilliant advert about the evils of toxic masculinity. This was encouraging, especially given that Gillette had made a fortune over the years by pretending there are differences between men and women. And although I never shave my body hair due to my feminist principles, I've started buying their razors anyway to support their valorous work.

Yes, Mary taught us to be vigilant when it comes to representation in the arts and advertising. But, in addition, we need to retrospectively censor anything from the past that might now be deemed problematic. As George Orwell once wrote in one of his motivational self-help books: 'Who controls the past controls the future.'

If you've ever been unfortunate enough to read any of the works of dead white males like Henry James, Leo Tolstoy or George Eliot, you'll be shocked at the lack of diversity. I recently read *Oliver Twist*, a so-called 'classic' by a male called Charles Dickens (written on white paper, no less), and there were literally no pangender or non-binary characters, or even the most fleeting reference to a mosque. Even the font had a certain heteronormative quality about it.

And we mustn't stop at fiction. As Nebal Maysaud noted in an article for the *New Music USA* website: 'Classical music is inherently racist.' There isn't a symphony in the world that wouldn't be improved by the addition of a bongo backbeat.

Gradually, we are making amends. Recently a coin commemorating the children's novelist Enid Blyton was cancelled by the Royal Mint because she held the kind of reactionary views about race, gender and sexuality that have long been deemed unacceptable. The fact that she was born in 1897 is absolutely no excuse for her failure to live up to the standards of twenty-first century intersectionalists. In fact, if you take an excerpt of an Enid Blyton book translated into German, and put it next to an excerpt from *Mein Kampf*, it looks exactly the same. Especially if, like me, you can't read German.

Likewise, in the light of recent revelations I have burned all of my albums by R. Kelly and Michael Jackson. They're all on Spotify anyway.

So in Mary's name let us go forth and censor. As she put it: 'Bad language coarsens the whole quality of our life. It normalises harsh, often indecent language, which despoils our communication.' Today we call this 'hate speech', a crime for which the death penalty ought to be reinstated. Militant state control of citizens' speech is a small price to pay to enforce a tolerant society.

As Mary once said: 'Words are like pineapples. They have the capacity to nourish, but can likewise cause serious harm if carelessly thrown about.'

ELIZABETH WARREN

SQUAW

Once upon a time there was a Native American woman called Elizabeth who decided to run for president of the United States. If she had succeeded, Elizabeth would have doubtless brought her charming indigenous traditions to the White House. She would have been the first Commander-in-Chieftain, known to all as 'Fiddles With Facts'.

Unfortunately, Elizabeth failed to secure the nomination because the Democratic party is apparently full of misogynists. This was a tragedy, as she was the most progressive candidate the party had ever seen. When it came to her commitment to wokeness, she could rival even Canadian Prime Minister Justin Trudeau. (It is true that Trudeau seemed to spend more time in blackface than out of it, but this was because he was transracial and born in the wrong skin.)

Elizabeth was the first ever presidential hopeful to announce her pronouns, which turned out to be 'she' and 'her'. Up until this point her pronouns had been a mystery, and most people simply referred to her as

When the blood in your veins returns to the sea, and the earth in your bones returns to the ground, perhaps then you will remember that this land does not belong to you, it is you who belong to this land.

ELIZABETH WARREN

'that' or 'it'. In addition, her preferred adverbs were 'briskly' and 'authoritatively', and her preferred adjectives were 'formidable' and 'moist'.

On the campaign trail she met a nine-year-old trans child who, she decided, should be granted the power to veto the appointment of a new Secretary of Education. After the disaster of Donald Trump, Elizabeth knew that the best way to restore the dignity of the White House was to ensure that important political decisions were left to prepubescents.

She was determined to fight for equality, close the gender pregnancy gap and, most significant of all, prevent Trump from seizing a second term in office. What America needed most of all was a female leader. Males could never lead a nation to prosperity given that their brains are marinated in testosterone. One might as well give the keys to the White House to a sack of dying sprats.

One of the saddest moments of Elizabeth's life came when she was forced to apologise for saying that she was Native American. Sadly, this was what it meant to be living in Trump's America, where ethnic minorities felt obliged to apologise simply because of who they were.

Even though the results of genetic testing had suggested that Elizabeth was only 1 / 1,024th Native

American, this was hardly surprising given that Cherokee DNA is notoriously evasive. The key point was that Elizabeth liked a drink and had a fondness for trinkets, which is all the evidence that anyone should have ever required.

In January 2019, Elizabeth was called upon to defend her people against a group of boys from Covington Catholic High School who had misbehaved on a trip to the Lincoln Memorial in Washington. A Native American activist called Nathan Phillips was surrounded by the jeering schoolboys, most of whom were wearing 'Make America Great Again' baseball caps. A clip of one boy, Nick Sandmann, was uploaded to the internet, and soon went viral. He was accused of 'smirking', an act of wanton violence.

Elizabeth took to social media to defend the victim. 'Omaha elder and Vietnam War veteran Nathan Phillips endured hateful taunts with dignity and strength,' she tweeted, sharing the footage to her millions of followers. Although the video had captured only a few minutes of the incident, Elizabeth knew in her heart that in addition to the smirking, the boys had chanted, flayed the old man's skin to make a wigwam, re-enacted the buffalo-hunt scene from *Dances With Wolves*, then displaced the entire Oglala Sioux Tribe from their reservation in South Dakota.

Even if this didn't happen, it only didn't happen in a purely non-metaphorical sense.

The MAGA hat was a symbol of everything that Elizabeth despised. As journalist David Klion noted: 'Wearing a MAGA hat is by definition a racist provocation and anyone who does it should be considered to be harassing any minorities in their general vicinity.' What was the first thing Hitler did before invading Poland? He put on a hat.

Needless to say, the only accessories that Elizabeth ever wore were buffalo-hide moccasins and beaded wampum belts.

DR VERONICA IVY

Once upon a time there was a woman called Veronica who was an internationally renowned doctor of cycling. As a baby she was christened Rhys McKinnon by accident, but this mistake was later corrected and she transitioned to the woman she always was: Rachel McKinnon.

Rachel later changed her name to Veronica Ivy, which was also always her name. Some lowlifes in the media continued to deadname her as 'Rachel', and others even double-deadnamed her as 'Rhys'. All of these people should obviously be arrested. She has always been Veronica Ivy, even when she was Rachel McKinnon (which she always was but now never has been) and *especially* when she was Rhys McKinnon (which she had never been even when she was). And if she changes her name again, she will always have been whatever name she decides to change it to.

I hope that's clear.

It was always obvious that Veronica was uncomfortable as a male, because she was never able to win

It's OK to be happy, even celebrate, when bad people die.

DR VERONICA IVY

any of her races. But as soon as she transitioned to female her confidence grew, and she triumphed at the UCI Masters Track Cycling World Championships. So much for female athletes being weaker.

Veronica was a catalyst for change in the sports world, which has long been dominated by bigotry. A recent article in the *Washington Post*, for instance, reported that Canadian researchers have discovered that 'dodgeball is a tool of oppression'. It's good to see these experts catching up with what social justice activists have known for years. With any luck, they'll now start looking into the blatant white supremacy of badminton.

In addition to her cycling feats, Veronica was a trans activist who wasn't afraid to take the moral high ground and wish misery and death upon those who disagreed with her politically. In August 2019 she took to social media to express her joy at the news that Magdalen Berns, a trans exclusionary radical feminist (TERF), had been diagnosed with brain cancer. When Berns died a few weeks later, Veronica bravely posted an image of a skeleton dancing on a grave.

For those who know so little about trans activism, this kind of gesture might seem a little callous. Similarly, there were many who took umbrage when

Veronica expressed her longing for cis people to 'die in a grease fire'. It's so distressing when those of us who seek to cultivate a society in which love and human kindness can flourish are misinterpreted as being a bunch of sociopathic cunts.

In spite of her enemies' slurs and mischaracterisations, Veronica became the most important trans icon since Ms. Pac-Man. Moreover, she was a fantastic role model for the young. Thanks to her example, children everywhere now know that you can still become a world-class athlete even if you are really bad at sports.

INTERLUDE: WHAT YOUR PARENTS WON'T TELL YOU ABOUT SEX

As you get older, you may begin to develop sexual feelings for other human beings. You might even find yourself attracted to plantlife, which is perfectly natural too. As a proud ecosexual, I make a point of displaying my sexual preference for vegetation wherever possible. I even run a kindergarten workshop in which I teach the kids how to write environmentally conscious slam poetry while I perform an act of eco-frottage with a cucumber vine. (I learnt this technique from a guru in Jaipur. He was very spiritual. He had a ring through his nose and everything.)

Sex education has long been a passion of mine, because I worry that the younger generation are being failed by the establishment. We know that this is true because even today the vast majority of young people grow up to be heterosexual. Something has gone seriously wrong.

Let me put this as bluntly as I can. Heterosexuality is a damaging power structure which must always be resisted unless it involves a female penis and a male vagina. All heterosexual sex is rape. Marriage is basically rape organised by a priest. With a disco.

So if you find yourself feeling attracted to the opposite sex, pay no heed. This is doubtless a phase, a fleeting perversion that can be overcome with a little self-discipline. And if you require further persuasion, just take a look at this:

GAY: **LEONARDO DA VINCI, ALAN TURING, VIRGINIA WOOLF**

STRAIGHT: **ROBERT MUGABE, HAROLD SHIPMAN, ADOLF HITLER**

I know whose side I'm on. Do you?

So let me break this down for y'all with a little bit of help from our old friend Dr Veronica Ivy. As an esteemed academic and professional cyclist, she has a way with words as well as a way with wheels. Here's an example of one of her tweets on the subject which should be incorporated into all school sex education curricula:

You: "I like dick"
Girl with dick says 'Hey, wanna date?'
"Oh . . . no . . . I only like dick on guys"

What your parents won't tell you about sex

Guy responds to date ad: 'Sup girl'
. . . guy has a vagina
"Oh, sorry, I only like guys with dicks"
Both cases trans people are left in the cold. 'Genital
* preferences' are transphobic.*

Veronica's eloquent words have taught us that any kind of sexual attraction based on biological sex is discriminatory. Just as heterosexuality is the most common form of homophobia, homosexuality is the most common form of transphobia. As Veronica says, pansexuality is the only acceptable sort of desire, and 'any sexual orientation other than pan is immoral'. And if you don't know what that means then you're nothing but a vile panphobe.

I repeat. Genitals have literally *nothing* to do with sexual attraction. In fact, if a straight man refuses to fellate a female penis, that just proves he's actually gay.

Now let's talk a little bit about gender and why it matters.

What does it mean to be male? What does it mean to be female? As it turns out, very little. As the political scientist and professor Roger Pielke Jr. has noted: 'There's no simple or even complex biological test you can apply that tells you who's a man and who's a woman.' The emphasis on research and data in the field of modern science is a disgrace. I have absolutely no desire to impregnate a male. But if I ever change my mind, I won't allow some 'scientist' to tell me that I can't.

The labels of 'male' and 'female' are solely a matter of identity, which is why it is absurd that professional archaeologists claim the power to determine the gender of ancient skeletons through scientific tests. Next they'll be telling us they can work out their pronouns by measuring the femurs.

As a young person, it is important that you understand that gender is a social construct designed by the patriarchy to impose a rigid hierarchy onto humankind. The gender binary is one of those myths that never actually existed, like male feminists, Islamic terrorism or Bruce Jenner. But if you're a boy who likes wearing dresses or a girl who likes football, you should probably transition immediately.

This might seem a little confusing, so I'll give a more specific example. For years I have been campaigning against the vile practice of dressing baby boys in blue and baby girls in pink, because there is nothing instinctively gender-based about colour preferences. At the same time, when my baby nephew seemed to favour a pink teddy rather than a blue one, this confirmed to me that he was actually a girl and I started slipping oestrogen supplements into his rusks.

Still confused? If so, it's because you've been taught to believe that contradictions are bad, whereas in fact they ought to be embraced. If you can't hold two seemingly incompatible ideas in your head at the same time then there's no way you can be an intersectional activist.

You're never too young to transition. We should never assume gender, even for the unborn. There isn't an ultrasound in the world that can as yet detect a non-binary foetus. And we can hardly expect an unborn child to announce their desire to transition. After all, it's very difficult to enunciate with a mouthful of amniotic fluid.

Recently a court in Texas ordered a father not to refer to one of his six-year-old twins as 'he', after his wife transitioned one child but not the other. Parents with identical twins would be well advised to follow this course of action. By transitioning just the one twin, not only can you help foster a more trans-inclusive home environment, but it'll be much easier to tell them apart. And if you have twins of different genders, they should probably both transition and simply swap their names and clothes.

81

The sort of ideas relating to gender and sexuality that you will be taught in biology lessons are so outdated that they are genuinely embarrassing to hear. Your teachers are likely to rely on a whole range of pseudo-sciences such as 'genetics', 'endocrinology' and 'facts'. If they'd bother to take even a basic course in Gender Studies they would realise that all of these superstitions have long been discredited.

But if you still require proof that the gender binary is over, here it is.

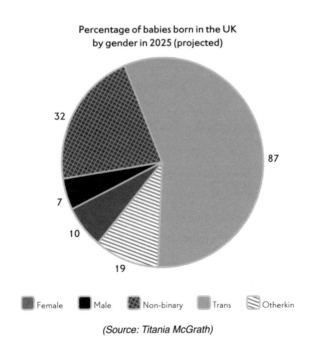

Percentage of babies born in the UK
by gender in 2025 (projected)

Female   Male   Non-binary   Trans   Otherkin

(Source: Titania McGrath)

I think that settles the matter once and for all.

And since gender is socially constructed, the best way to prove this is to construct as many new genders as possible. In our new woke era, there are an infinite number of genders to choose from. So if you don't fancy being a 'male' or 'female', here are some other options for you to consider:

- Agender
- Pangender
- Gender Nonconforming
- Unman
- Unwoman
- Demigirlboyman
- Genital Dissident
- Proxi-Male Femme-Adjacent
- Shabba Ranks
- Derelict Minge
- Neutrois
- MascuFem
- Non-binary
- Non non-binary
- Proxi non non-binary
- Proxi non non-binary adjacent
- Ghost Vulva
- Tugbucket
- Hirsute Winklepicker
- Boiled Elf

Above all, be sensitive when it comes to the language of gender and sexuality. Do not say the word 'bisexual' because that implies that there are only two sexes and is therefore transphobic. Instead of 'LGBTQIA+', therefore, you should say 'LGXTQIA+'. And avoid patriarchal terminology such as 'cum', 'jizz' or 'semen'; it's much better to simply call it 'hate syrup'.

JO SWINSON

POLITICIAN

Once upon a time there was a woman called Jo who was sick and tired of seeing old white males on the television shouting at each other in the Houses of Parliament. She decided she wanted to become the leader of a major political party. That didn't quite work out, so she joined the Liberal Democrats instead.

Jo hailed from a working-class area of the UK known as Scotland, where people tend to die young because of their lack of hygiene and fondness for heroin. But because Jo came from such humble origins, it meant that she would be able to understand the very people she would be lying to, which is an excellent skill for a politician.

When the British people voted on whether or not to leave the European Union (which is a sweet little club for all the left-wing world leaders who want to end capitalism by pretending to love it), Jo was very upset. This was because the population clearly didn't know what they were voting for. When they said they wanted

I can be the next Prime Minister.

JO SWINSON

to leave the EU, they didn't necessarily think that meant leaving the EU.

Try asking any Brexit supporter why they voted Leave. The answer is always the same: 'A bus told me to.'

So Jo decided to take over the Liberal Democrats and put a stop to Brexit. Back then, the party was being run by a man called Vince Cable, who was 104 years old. Jo realised that in order to rejuvenate their brand they would need somebody young and sexy. The last time Vince Cable had sex with anyone, they'd given him change in shillings.

Initially, Jo's plan was to push for a second Brexit referendum so that the population could be given another opportunity to vote the correct way. She considered it a broken kind of democracy that would allow a majority of voters to impose their wishes on the rest of us.

Many prominent millionaire celebrities supported her in this and called the project the 'People's Vote'. This was a very clever name, because it reminded everyone that the people hadn't really voted last time and that they had merely been doing the bidding of Russian bots on Facebook.

The millionaires all campaigned assiduously. They knew that a second referendum would go their way, so long as the following were no longer eligible to vote:

- The elderly
- The poor
- Northerners
- Any other racists not already covered by the above

But Jo soon realised that a lot of people wouldn't be happy with this arrangement, and so she changed her tactics and campaigned to rescind Brexit entirely. This proved that Jo was one of the few working-class people who understood the complexities of politics. Most of the others were more interested in traditional working-class pursuits, such as visiting music halls, eating jellied eels and thieving.

With Jo in charge, the Liberal Democrats went from strength to strength. She enjoyed railing against the 'white men stuck in the past' who ran the country. And although criticising people for their skin colour isn't technically 'liberal', and trying to overturn the result of a national referendum isn't technically 'democratic', under Jo's leadership the party's name stayed the same. After all, the 'Illiberal Antidemocrats' isn't quite so catchy.

In spite of all this, Jo somehow lost her seat in the 2019 general election. The electorate got it wrong *again*.

Typical.

BRIE LARSON

SUPERHEROINE

Once upon a time there was an actor called Brie who played the lead role in the Hollywood blockbuster *Captain Marvel*. It was undoubtedly the best movie of all time, an unmitigated masterpiece, a triumph of feminist valour over the twitching remnants of a dying patriarchy. I can't wait to see it.

Brie was well known for her commitment to social justice. In an interview for *Marie Claire*, she noted that the critics who reviewed her films were over-whelmingly white and male, and so she insisted that her press tour for *Captain Marvel* should be more inclusive. (I have decided to follow her lead on this. As such, white male critics do *not* have my consent to review this book. In addition, any bad reviews will be considered a hate crime.)

Brie was lauded in the press as the first major female Hollywood action star. Feminists around the world breathed a sigh of relief that *finally* they had the powerful role model they had always craved. With the exception of Sigourney Weaver, Linda

I don't really have any people in my
life who aren't gypsies.

BRIE LARSON

Hamilton, Pam Grier, Geena Davis, Michelle Yeoh, Angelina Jolie, Uma Thurman, Jennifer Lopez, Halle Berry, Sandra Bullock, Julianne Moore, Kathleen Turner and all the other women who had played leading roles in action movies, Brie Larson was literally the first woman ever to play a leading role in an action movie.

As Brie knew all too well, this was because women in fiction have for ever been mere instruments by which male writers could justify female subjugation and cisnormative genito-imperialism. The very first female character, Eve from the Garden of Eden, was portrayed as a naked harridan who enjoyed scrumping at the behest of reptiles.

Similarly, the lack of queer representation in popular cinema has been a major problem since the dawn of Hollywood. A lesbian kiss in *Star Wars: The Rise of Skywalker* amounted to approximately two seconds of screen time. The one gay character in *Avengers: Endgame* was unnamed and barely appeared at all. The very least we could have seen was Iron Man being double-penetrated by Thor and the Hulk.

But thanks to trailblazers like Brie, Hollywood became fully feminist and intersectional. No longer were female characters merely present for the purposes of sexual objectification. First came the all-female

Ghostbusters reboot, which was extremely popular with everyone except for the general public. Then there was the new *Charlie's Angels* film, which flopped at the box office, once again proving that cinemagoers would rather be 'entertained' than be taught about the importance of social justice. But this was precisely the kind of regressive mindset that activists like Brie were struggling against.

These examples have taught us that the more money a movie makes the less likely it is to be woke. This means that the mark of a film's success is how few people want to see it.

Brie went on to be nominated for an Oscar for her role in the movie *Room*, and in the same year posted a message of support on Instagram for the #OscarsSoWhite hashtag, which was a campaign which pointed out the injustice of an awards ceremony that has too many white nominees. Brie must have been appalled when she won, but generously accepted it anyway in the name of the minorities she liked to defend.

Brie longed for a time that the Oscars would become truly intersectional. This would involve scrapping all the old award categories in favour of new ones. These could include:

- Most feminist film
- Most woke screenplay
- Least predatory male
- Gayest sound editing
- Fattest supporting Filipino
- Bravest vegan in a transblack role

With luminaries like Brie on the case, this might one day become a reality.

SAM SMITHS

MUSICIAN

Once upon a time there was a singer called Sam whose sex was randomly assigned as 'male' at birth. I think the obstetrician must have flipped a coin or something.

As Sam was later to discover, they was actually non-binary. They had always known that they was neither male nor female. In a video they posted on social media, they was seen discussing the 'vivacious woman' inside of them while dancing seductively and pouting, which is what all women do.

So in September 2019, they announced that their pronouns were they/them. It was important to Sam to show everybody how interesting and unique them was because nobody seemed to find their music particularly memorable, apart from the one that they borrowed from Tom Petty. If you asked the average person to name some of their songs, you could probably count the result on one of Abu Hamza's hands.

Sam would announce their pronouns to just about anyone – journalists, waiters, passers-by – only to find

I've made my music so that it could
be about anything and everybody –
whether it's a guy, a female or a goat
– and everybody can relate to that.

SAM SMITHS

that in most cases they didn't break out into sponta-
neous applause. This kind of harassment was exactly
why Sam had the police on speed dial.

Reactions to Sam's announcement were mixed;
their fans were ecstatic, but many in the media were
nonplussed. Some even claimed that Sam's use of
'they' as singular might cause grammatical confusion.
They preferred to call them him and they were
annoyed at them because they did not respect their
right to choose their pronouns for themself.

Less than a week after Sam's announcement, the
Merriam-Webster dictionary decided to add the
gender-neutral 'they' pronoun to their list of official
words. Even though the traditional role of the dictionary was to record common usage, and even though
very few people recognised 'they' as anything other
than a plural pronoun, the staff at Merriam-Webster
were sufficiently enlightened to ignore all of that. That
said, their dictionary still defines 'woman' as 'adult
female person' and 'man' as 'adult male human', so it
clearly still has some vestigial transphobia.

Such was the impact of Sam's coming out as non-
binary that Merriam-Webster made the singular 'they'
its word of the year for 2019. This was reminiscent of
when the Oxford dictionary made 'youthquake' the
word of the year in 2017 in reference to the sudden

surge of political activism among left-leaning teen-agers. Although this was probably the first and last time the word was ever used, it did help to cement the Oxford dictionary's progressive credentials.

Sam Smiths deserves our respect. They is a hero.

TOMÁS DE TORQUEMADA

O nce upon a time there was a man called Tomás who established an official institution of social justice known as the 'Spanish Inquisition' to inquire into 'scientists' who insisted on 'proclaiming' their hateful 'ideas' about the 'world'. When presidential candidate Joe Biden declared: 'We choose truth over facts,' he was quoting one of Tomás's most powerful maxims.

Tomás was perfect for the job of rooting out heresy, because he was naturally suspicious of everyone and everything. He was the sort of person who would unfold a calzone before eating it.

During his time as Grand Inquisitor it was estimated that Tomás burned approximately two thousand heretics to death. This might seem harsh, but when you consider that some of these people were saying incredibly offensive things you can see why he felt there was little alternative. He was one of the earliest activists to recognise that failure to comply with the truth only served to destabilise social

You'd better sing like a canary or I'll chew your balls off.

TOMÁS DE TORQUEMADA

cohesion. To put it simply, he tortured and burned people out of love.

Tomás laid the groundwork for today's 'cancel culture', an important strategy by which we might purge society of those who express bad thoughts. Think of the likes of Roseanne Barr, Jeremy Clarkson, Megyn Kelly, or that insufferable ferret PewDiePie. Tomás would have had no hesitation in incinerating such problematic individuals. Of course, I am not for one moment suggesting that this would be something I'd support, but it would certainly make our society considerably more inclusive.

Many historians have been unkind to Tomás on the grounds that he was opposed to free speech. But this was precisely what made him so ahead of his time. As any woke activist will tell you, free speech is a tool used by fascists to spread hate. A kind of hate spatula, if you will.

People always go on and on about the importance of free speech, but when I say that it should be illegal to express offensive ideas I'm told to shut up. This is a clear case of double standards.

In any case, the concept of freedom of speech originated in Ancient Greece around the end of the fifth century BC, so even by the time of Tomás's birth in 1420 it was already outdated.

Tomás de Torquemada

It's time for a new Inquisition. We've heard enough from alt-right edgelords, comedians and satirists, TERFs and SWERFs, and anyone else who insists on asking difficult questions. If Tomás were alive today, he'd be setting up online petitions to strengthen hate-speech laws and campaigning for tighter controls on internet freedom. As committed left-wing activists, our priority must be to ensure that corporations in Silicon Valley are empowered to set the limits of what we can and cannot say.

As Tomás so memorably put it: 'hate speech isn't possible without free speech, so if you're defending free speech that's basically hate speech'.

NELSON MANDELA

Once upon a time there was a man called Nelson who was put in prison for being black and then escaped and became king. Or something.

Nelson was born and raised in Africa, which is one of the poorest countries in the world. You can tell how poor it is because it is literally full of ethnic minorities. I was there for part of my gap year, and it was so bleak. The locals were a delight, although I haven't posted any images of them on Instagram because they didn't strike me as particularly photogenic.

I even got a tapeworm from drinking the local water, because they don't have Evian. I wasn't prepared to kill off the tapeworm because I'm a militant vegan. Also, worms are non-binary so they've suffered enough. It's still in my intestines actually. I call it Bernice. And Bernice is free to live there in comfort until Bernice decides to leave of *their* own free will.

Nelson was born in a town called Mvezo, which must have been hard for him because it's so difficult to pronounce. He was a humble villager (probably) who

They have wings but cannot fly. They're birds that think they're fish. And every year, they embark on a nearly impossible journey to find a mate.

NELSON MANDELA

would have grown up with lots of other humble villagers who liked to go fishing in cute little boats and balance urns on their heads. They may not understand the difference between a Merlot and a Pinot Noir, or the correct fork to use for a peach-and-pancetta salad, but my God they know how to snag a decent catfish.

To be honest, I don't know all that much about Nelson because I haven't done any research. But I know he spent a long time in prison, and that he narrated the hit movie *March of the Penguins*. And all this in spite of the fact that it's notoriously difficult for people of colour to break the glass ceiling and become fully fledged celebrities. Just consider how quickly famous black people fade from the public consciousness. When was the last time you ever heard anyone talking about Floella Benjamin, Lonnie Gordon or Mr. T? Chaka Khan can only get work these days by pretending to be a drag version of herself.

On the downside, Nelson was allegedly heterosexual. But men who are attracted to women clearly have feminine tastes and are therefore probably gay.

I feel a particular affinity for Nelson, because I was once suspended from Twitter for a whole day. The experience was traumatic and lasting, and helped me to understand how he must have felt. If anything, my ordeal was even more damaging. Nelson may have had to endure decades of incarceration, but at least his male privilege protected him from ever having to put up with mansplaining, or being subject to wolf-whistling by grubby proles on a building site.

DESMOND IS AMAZING

DRAG KID

Once upon a time there was a drag kid called Desmond is Amazing who started performing in bars when he was only eleven years old. This was empowering not just for him, but also for the adults who used to throw money at him to show their support.

The left-wing press rightly praised Desmond as a trailblazer for drag kids everywhere. *Out* magazine called him a 'rainbow of positivity'. The *Huffington Post* described him as 'inspiring'. Drag queens are ideal role models for young children. Especially for those who dream of one day making a career out of lip-syncing to Donna Summer.

Inevitably, the boomers started whinging about Desmond's success. But then, old people are super fucking problematic. They don't know what 'sapio-sexual' means, most of them aren't vegan and they're not on Instagram (which means we can't be sure what they're up to). Even the ones who fought in the Second World War ended up voting for Brexit, so we can be

My mom doesn't like me
drinking caffeine.

DESMOND IS AMAZING

fairly certain they were only opposing Hitler as a cover for their fascism.

And of course the conservatives all crawled out of the woodwork to complain about how disturbing they found Desmond's performances. This was because, as stuffy reactionaries, they had convinced themselves that there was something inappropriate about a child pretending to snort ketamine and gyrating on a podium for tips.

In fact, drag queens have always been subversive artists who are able to deconstruct the notion of typical feminine stereotypes by dressing up in massive wigs, high heels, excessive make-up and large fake breasts. They have become important mentors for small children, and even the BBC has promoted 'Drag Queen Story Time' in which drag artists use 'diverse storytelling to connect kids with LGBT+ role-models of colour'. For my part, I've started running school workshops on how to decolonise your BDSM leather and latex fetish activities.

The vast majority of infants are woke. When my brother recently tried to read J. M. Barrie's *Peter Pan* to his five-year-old daughter, she slammed the book shut, threw it to the floor, and shouted: 'NO – MORE – WHITE – MALE – CHARACTERS!' There was a long, terse silence before she took herself off to bed. They haven't spoken since.

This is hardly surprising. As the stunning work of Desmond is Amazing shows, children these days are far more concerned about diversity and representation than exciting characters or interesting plotlines. Even the latest range of Barbie dolls includes those with wheelchairs, prosthetic limbs, braided hair, hijabs and diverse body types.

That said, until I see a mixed-race HIV-positive translesbian doll carrying an Antifa flag I'm not really interested.

INTERLUDE: HOW TO SAVE THE WORLD

I joined climate activist group Extinction Rebellion last year because I care about the environment and I wanted to meet Emma Thompson. But in recent months there has been a horrific backlash against our fearless work. We all saw that footage circulating online of an Extinction Rebellion protester being dragged from the top of a Tube train by commuters. That's the thing about fascists: they always want the trains to run on time.

Other complaints have arisen from people who allegedly experienced disruption while they were trying to 'get to work' (whatever that means) or going into hospital for 'cancer treatment'. Don't these selfish miscreants understand that the apocalypse is upon us? The ice caps are shrinking, the trees are almost extinct, and I haven't seen an ocelot for ages.

Climate change causes erratic weather conditions, which is really bad for the hedge maze on my estate. This is why I like to be extra cautious when it comes to my carbon footprint. For instance, I always make sure that at least one of my cars is energy efficient.

And whenever I fly in Daddy's private jet I usually ask Nenita to plant a few extra begonias in the herbaceous border.

So what can we do about it? The truth is that the Earth's fate lies in the hands of people like you: the youth. It should be compulsory for anyone under the age of sixteen to be a member of our movement. You are the generation who are going to be forced to live without an ozone layer, which is going to make sunbathing really problematic.

And then there will be the inevitable food shortages. As activist Gail Bradbrook recently pointed out on *Good Morning Britain*, her two children 'won't have enough food to eat in a few years'. This strikes me as an understatement. I wouldn't be surprised if they gradually chew each other to death.

It isn't just a matter of preventing Armageddon. As the movement's co-founder Stuart Basden wrote in a recent article, Extinction Rebellion is also about defeating white supremacy, the patriarchy, Eurocentrism, heteronormativity and class hierarchy. So if your parents claim that they find it too difficult to be green, tell them that they can still show their support by having gay sex with a few African peasants.

Our tactics in Extinction Rebellion are varied, but for the most part we like to glue or chain ourselves to things and strip naked. We tend to attach ourselves to famous landmarks, buses and even the occasional homeless person.

We have three main aims. Firstly, the government and the media need to start telling the truth about climate change. There is so little discussion on this topic that most people haven't even heard of the climate, let alone realise that it's changing. I only found out about it because I watched the film *Highlander II*, which depicts a dystopian future where the ozone layer has fully depleted. Sean Connery plays a Spaniard with a Scottish accent and Christopher Lambert plays a Scotsman who sounds French. Is that really the kind of perverted future we want for our children?

Secondly, we must reduce greenhouse-gas emissions to net zero by the year 2025. Critics have pointed out that the restrictions on key industries that would be required in order to achieve this would cause economic meltdown and that the poorest in our society would be most severely impacted. But hardly any working-class people ever turn up to our protests, which surely means that they're not bothered either way.

Finally, the government must outsource all decisions relating to ecological issues to a citizens' assembly. It is perfectly obvious that our current system of representative democracy is failing and that our politicians cannot be trusted. We need to restore power to the people, who are always right about what is best for the country. (Except when it comes to Brexit, in which case they should have been ignored.)

As for those who claim that the coronavirus crisis has shown that there are far greater threats to humanity than climate change, I would simply say this. Humanity *is* the threat. But if you are concerned about the apocalyptic potential of global pandemics, it would be a good idea to urge all straight white males to self-isolate.

Not because of the coronavirus, but because they're so fucking annoying.

POPE JOAN

MALE IMPERSONATOR

Once upon a time there was a woman called Joan who sought to dismantle the patriarchy from within. There were many male-dominated institutions to choose from – given that this was the ninth century and the gender pay gap was almost as bad as it is today – but she eventually decided to target the Catholic Church and become the first, and last, female Pope.

The first thing that Joan had to do was to convince the priests and bishops at the Vatican that she was male. She achieved this by catcalling, groping, interrupting women, playing *Grand Theft Auto*, brawling in pubs, spitting, shouting and aggressively spreading her legs on public transport.

Everyone was fooled, and Joan was duly elected to the papacy. It is extremely ironic that militant feminists often make the best male impersonators. The reason for this remains a conundrum.

Joan got away with it for years, challenging the exegetes of the Vatican at every opportunity on the bigotry of the Bible. Why, Joan would ask, is there no

Chromosomes are a social construct.

POPE JOAN

non-binary vegan representation in either the Old or New Testament? Why is the Whore of Babylon so flagrantly slut-shamed? Why does it say that whenever a woman is on her period she has to isolate herself for seven days and then give some pigeons to a priest (Leviticus 15:19–29)? Leaving aside the misogyny for one moment, it's notoriously difficult to catch pigeons when you're suffering from menstrual cramps.

In addition, Joan would subtly introduce new passages into the Bible when nobody was looking in order to promote LGBT rights. For instance, she added a few cruising tips for gay men who were interested in sex tourism: 'Egyptian men have members the size of donkeys, and ejaculate violently like wild stallions' (Ezekiel 23:20). Very few of the faithful seemed to notice, as for some reason this verse wasn't generally read out during sermons.

Joan would also challenge the way in which Jesus was always depicted as white in the various artworks on display in Rome. It was bad enough that the figurehead of the one true church was some kind of zombie incel, but nobody was going to buy the idea that a Palestinian could look so downright Celtic.

Joan's secret was eventually discovered when, during a procession through Vatican City, she gave birth to a child. This was centuries before trans activists had explained to everyone that pregnancy was not exclusively a female condition, so suspicions were immediately aroused.

There's no getting around the fact that Joan had made a foolish blunder. If you're pretending to be a man, and are heavily pregnant and experiencing uterine contractions, some would say this isn't the optimal moment to participate in a public procession. You'd call in sick, wouldn't you?

As historian E. R. Chamberlain notes, even 'as late as 1600, a bust of *Johannes VIII, femina ex Anglia* was unquestioningly accepted among the row of papal busts that glare out over the heads of worshippers in Siena Cathedral'. But scholars have since argued that there was no such individual as Pope Joan, and that she was the invention of anti-papal propagandists of the Renaissance. This is because our history has been written by misogynists. It is in their interests to elide powerful women from the annals of the past.

Just because Pope Joan may have not existed, that does *not* make it OK to erase her identity or her key contribution to the feminist cause.

LINDA SARSOUR

ISLAMOFEMINIST

O nce upon a time there was a woman called Linda who co-organised the first ever 'Women's March' after the election of Donald Trump. This was a fantastic event where we all joined together to protest against the ongoing degradation of women by dressing up as giant vaginas.

As a lifelong pro-feminist and pro-Islam activist, Linda understood that the Koran was a feminist book and that the part about beating women was clearly ironic. Unlike Jesus Christ and his dozen henchmen, the Prophet Muhammad had a terrific sense of humour.

Linda wore her hijab with pride, and whenever she encountered Muslim women who left their hair uncovered her heart would break for their internalised Islamophobia. It's important to remember that whenever someone says that Muslim women should reject the veil, they are clearly a bigot who wants to see them get sunburned. Personally, I was thrilled to see hijabs in the recent swimsuit issue of *Sports*

You'll know when you're living
under Shariah law if suddenly all
your loans and credit cards become
interest-free. Sound nice, doesn't it?

LINDA SARSOUR

Illustrated. If women are to be sexually objectified, the least we can do is ensure they dress with modesty.

One thing that Linda knew for sure was that the US was the least progressive country in the world. Consider the following statistics:

ANTI-GAY HATE CRIMES RECORDED BY POLICE IN 2019	
SAUDI ARABIA	0
PAKISTAN	0
YEMEN	0
BRUNEI	0
SOMALIA	0
AFGHANISTAN	0
UNITED STATES OF AMERICA	1,404

And yet some still claim that it's the Islamic states that are homophobic. The data speaks for itself.

Linda was an avid supporter of Sharia Law and worked strenuously to raise awareness of everyday Islamophobia. This problem is far more prevalent than people generally realise. Only the other day I saw a gay couple sharing a ham sandwich in an Uber. Airline security staff are also notoriously Islamophobic; if you don't believe me, try shouting 'Allāhu Akbar' at an airport and see what happens.

And last summer, a man was sacked from his job at the supermarket chain Asda for sharing a clip online of the comedian Billy Connolly mocking Islam. Thank goodness there are still some brave supermarkets out there who are willing to uphold medieval blasphemy laws.

Linda had a way with words, but was often misinterpreted. When she called for a 'jihad' against the president, she wasn't talking about the kind of jihad that involved violence, but the kind of jihad that involved posting a series of robust tweets.

And when she said that she wished she could take away the vagina of activist Ayaan Hirsi Ali, she was cleverly using aggressively misogynistic language to demonstrate how progressive and kind she was. As always, right-wingers in the media were up to their old tricks of twisting her words to resemble what she actually said.

Linda's brand of feminism was unapologetically intersectional. 'If you are in a movement and you are not following a woman of colour,' she once said, 'you are in the wrong movement'. This is why I have withdrawn my support for the British Red Cross, the Make a Wish Foundation and the Royal Society for the Prevention of Cruelty to Animals, all of which have white males in charge. If these organisations can't make the effort to embrace intersectional politics, then quite frankly they can suck my black dick.

Eventually the organisers of the Women's March cut ties with Linda, partly due to ongoing controversy over her links with Louis Farrakhan, a man who had compared Jews to termites. What they failed to understand is that termites are actually very industrious, so if anything this was a compliment.

MAHATMA GANDHI

PACIFIST

Once upon a time there was a man called Mohandas who decided to call himself 'Mahatma' instead because it was Sanskrit for 'great-souled'. Yes, he really was that pretentious. (I'll admit that I went through a phase of referring to myself as 'Saviour of the Downtrodden', but I was only twelve and it didn't really catch on.)

In fact, I'm only including this chapter because my publishers insisted. 'How can you write a book on history's greatest pioneers of social justice without including Gandhi?' they shrieked from their ivory boardrooms. To be honest, I'm sick of hearing about him. I mean, I'm sure if I'd grown up with Mahatma's degree of male privilege I could have invented India too.

But I suppose I'd better focus on the positives. Well, for a start Mahatma was a vegan. He was quoted as saying: 'I will not take milk, milk-products or meat. If not taking these things should mean my death, I feel I'd rather face it.' In fact, his veganism is almost

It's not OK to be white.

MAHATMA GANDHI

certainly the aspect of his character for which he will be best remembered. Ever since Charles Darwin discovered that all living creatures are related, it's basically been a choice between veganism or canni- balism. A no-brainer, really.

Mahatma understood that all animals are naturally vegan. The 'food chain' is a myth fabricated by men to justify eating meat. If cats and dogs weren't exposed to the influence of mass media, they'd probably only eat turnips.

But Mahatma was also an incredibly witty individ- ual. One particularly revealing exchange took place during his visit to the UK in 1931 when he was due to meet King George V. A journalist approached him and asked: 'Mr Gandhi, do you think you are properly dressed to meet the king?' Mahatma simply retorted: 'Do not worry about my clothes. The King has enough clothes on for both of us.' Not many people are aware that Mahatma was actually quite the little bitch. His put-downs were notoriously waspish and acerbic. He was very much like an Asian Kenneth Williams.

The only other good thing about Mahatma was that he has inspired a new generation of eco-warriors. He never used plastic straws, didn't bother with deodorant, and he didn't even own a fridge. Moreover, the entire modus operandi of the Extinction Rebellion movement is based on his principle of 'non-violent resistance'. Mahatma's followers used to call this '*satyagraha*', because they lacked the necessary discipline to learn English properly.

Mahatma was eventually assassinated. Tragic as this might be, he'd had a long life. He was born premature, so that's an extra two weeks already.

Ultimately, the combination of my social justice advocacy and my courageous environmental activism means that I have far surpassed anything that Mahatma ever achieved. He might have brought the British empire to its knees, but did he ever glue himself to the Docklands Light Railway, stripped to the waist and smeared in woad? No, he was too busy mincing around in flip-flops and collecting salt.

JESSICA YANIV

Once upon a time there was a beautiful and brave trans woman called Jessica who laboured with every fibre of her being to fight for equal rights. She did this principally by taking female beauticians to court if they refused to wax her balls.

She was right to do so. In a supposedly enlightened and progressive age, it is outrageous that trans women cannot force other women to touch their scrotums. As Jessica repeatedly asserted, trans women are women. The word 'trans', therefore, is utterly redundant. This means that the phrase 'trans women' is actually transphobic. Even the word 'transphobic' is transphobic because it contains the transphobic word 'trans'.

This really isn't difficult.

Jessica was a leading activist in the LGBTQ2SIA movement. This is not to be confused with the LGBTQQIP2SAA movement or the LGBTQIA+ movement: these are groups of bigoted dissidents who need to be cancelled.

At least my pussy is tight and not loose after pushing out a ten-pound baby.

JESSICA YANIV

It didn't take long for Jessica to build up a mass following on Twitter, with no less than 140,000 people eager to be updated with her progressive declarations. Critics accused her of buying fake followers on the grounds that they appeared to be mostly inactive, but that was because they were all so oppressed by the cisgender heteropatriarchy that they lacked the energy even to occasionally hit the retweet icon.

Jessica described herself as a 'lesbian warrior princess', which if anything underplays her contribution to our valiant struggle. She would often experience painful period pains in her female penis, which made the important process of waxing even more arduous. Under such circumstances, the salon workers who refused her request were not simply acting in a discriminatory way, they were anti-trans guerrillas.

During the trial, many commentators expressed concern that Jessica had apparently posted anti-immigrant messages on social media. This was deemed relevant because most of those being sued were foreign people of colour. Inevitably, Jessica's words had been taken completely out of context. When she wrote that immigrants 'aren't exactly the cleanest people' she was merely expressing concern for the hygiene of those who live in countries with poor sanitation. In this, as in all things, Jessica's benevolence knew no bounds.

Then came the accusations that Jessica had a fetish for young girls, simply because she had mentioned helping them with their tampons in a series of Facebook messages. There were allegations of predatory actions in her past, all of which came out during the trial. What these accusers failed to realise is that Jessica had only behaved in this way *before* she transitioned to female. Jessica has always been female, so how could she possibly be held accountable for the toxic masculinity of the male she never was?

HILLARY CLINTON

GRANDMOTHER

Once upon a time there was a grandmother called Hillary who was destined to become president of the United States of America. All the polls predicted her success, and *Newsweek* even went so far as to print a special commemorative edition with the cover line: 'Madam President: Hillary Clinton's historic journey to the White House'. 125,000 copies eventually had to be recalled once the news broke that the electorate had made a mistake. We can't even be certain that they were recycled.

The failure of the American people to elect Hillary confirmed that they could not be trusted when it came to making important decisions. Hillary was so angry that she boycotted her own concession speech, which she was expected to deliver on election night. Instead, she sent her campaign manager John Podesta to explain that she was a bit busy and would get around to it eventually. Critics claimed that this was a churlish act, but surely she was showing utmost respect for the democratic process by postponing her speech until she sobered up.

We are the president.
HILLARY CLINTON

But why did Hillary lose? It makes absolutely no sense, given that she had run such an excellent election campaign. One of her finest moments was when she pointed out that many of those who supported Donald Trump were 'deplorables', which for some reason didn't help to persuade them of her point of view. After Hillary lost, many of us on the left took time to reflect on why we had failed to win over the public. After much soul-searching, we reached the obvious conclusion: we didn't call them racist often enough.

Some claimed that Hillary lost simply because she lacked charisma, was a corporate shill, and enjoyed killing lawyers. Others put it down to her supposed 'gaffes'. In March 2016, for instance, she annoyed some plebs in Ohio by claiming that she was planning to 'put a lot of coal miners and coal companies out of business'. This was taken by many to signify that she had contempt for ordinary working people, but this is nonsense. Most of her domestic staff were working class, and she had a fantastic relationship with some of them. She would even let them have every other weekend off so long as the pelmets were properly dusted.

After the results came in, feminists were horrified to learn that 53 per cent of American women had voted for Trump, which showed that internalised misogyny was an even greater problem than we had assumed. These women didn't seem to understand that they would only achieve true independence once they learned to accept the decisions that intersectional feminists made for them.

In spite of the pleas of activists, women had neglected to 'vote with their vaginas'. Worse still, some had taken the advice literally, which caused no end of bother for those who had to clean up the voting booths after the polls had closed.

Ultimately, anyone who voted for Trump was either racist, fascist, sexist, homophobic, or was hypnotised by Vladimir Putin. As such, we can ignore their votes and positively declare that Hillary Clinton won the election. She *is* the president, no matter what the media says. My lived experience tells me that it is so.

JOSEPH STALIN

STALINIST

O nce upon a time there were two white male fascists called Adolf Hitler and Winston Churchill whose toxic masculinity was so pronounced that they decided to start a war. Everyone got involved, except for Switzerland who were too busy making chocolate. But one man decided that he needed to stand up to the fascist threat. That man was Joseph Stalin.

Joseph was passionate about social justice. He participated in the Russian revolution in 1905 in order to oppose the patriarchy. And he popularised the writings of Karl Marx, one of history's most famous and heavily bearded intersectional feminists.

Stalin's time as leader of the Soviet Union was the most productive period in the country's history. His programmes of modernisation led to the expansion of the coal, oil and steel industries and a booming economy. Those who refused to sign up to Joseph's new ideas tended to die young, which just proves that communism saves lives.

140

Trotsky was a fake ass bitch who got what he deserved.

JOSEPH STALIN

Capitalists always accused Joseph of being a 'tyrant' because they were jealous of his success. They alleged that he rounded up gay people and put them into 'concentration camps', but he only did this because he was trying to create a safe space for the queer experience. Che Guevara used to do a similar thing. (Che was the great Marxist revolutionary who launched a popular line of T-shirts. I have a few in mauve.)

Joseph's camps were known as 'gulags', and they were places where people could learn about social justice. As the LGBTQ group at Goldsmiths University Student Union pointed out, these were 'compassionate' and 'educational' environments with 'regular classes, book clubs, newspaper editorial teams, sports, theatre and performance groups'. And they got all of this for free. What the hell were they bitching about?

Yes, a few of them starved to death – records suggest 1,053,829 in a twenty-year period – but a short life is a small price to pay for someone who enjoys all the advantages of white privilege. It isn't possible for white people to be oppressed, because they occupy positions of power and benefit from the structural racism that they perpetuate by virtue of their whiteness. And yes, that also goes for Russian peasants who refuse to listen to their betters.

Admittedly, Joseph had a temper. He massacred a few thousand Poles, sanctioned mass rape, and assassinated a pig called Snowball. But in spite of these blunders, his greatest legacy was to prove that communism *works*. We should campaign assiduously to emulate his example and achieve a new socialist utopia. And with the added benefits of modern air conditioning, double glazing, and perhaps one or two water features, we can ensure that the gulags are even better this time around.

CONCLUSION

When I told my friends that I was thinking of writing a book for kids, they almost choked on their vegan tartines. For some reason, they were under the impression that I despise children. It is true that I have occasionally called for the decriminalisation of infanticide, but that's only because of my opposition to heteronormativity and the very principle of reproduction. This isn't really a problem for me anyway, as I've had my ovaries removed for an installation art piece.

However, in the process of writing this book I have realised that there is much to be said for the younger generation. I now understand that, as children, you are victims of the oppressive fascistic system under which we all live. Never forget that you didn't consent to be born. Your very conception was an act of rape. Your parents, therefore, are rapists.

But you have no need for these 'biological' mothers and fathers. In the course of these pages I have presented the very finest woke role models for you to emulate, all far superior to any of those ageing frauds who happen to share your DNA.

And yet, I have left out perhaps the most important role model of all.

Me.

I may be a simple Kensington girl with a modest trust fund and a thirst for justice, but it is my destiny to guide your generation to a new world order. I'm like a younger, hotter, female version of the Pied Piper of Hamelin, and you are my rats.

This book has been the first tentative step on your long journey towards radical intersectional activism. If you follow my advice, you too can be a brave champion for justice. Like whoever it was who killed Hitler.

You can start at school. If you are serious about social justice it is imperative that you pressurise your teaching staff into eliminating books written by straight white males. If all your classmates rebel at the same time, the school authorities will have no choice but to capitulate. And when they do so, you should have all the offensive books burned in the playground so that everyone can see what happens when fascists try to spread their wicked ideology.

You must embrace feminism and reject heteronormativity. This means that you need to recognise that heterosexuality was invented by patriarchs as a means to justify their subjugation of women. Men serve absolutely no function in today's society. Given the fact that some women have wombs, and some trans women have testicles, surely we've reached the point where we no longer require men in order to exist as a species?

The very worst thing that can happen to you is to get pregnant. The phenomenon of pregnancy has produced some of the most disordered people in history. Some of the more notable by-products of pregnancy include: Jeffrey Dahmer, Ted Bundy, Albert Fish and the Beast of Jersey. Many of my friends who became mothers have told me that they could feel their unborn sons kicking from within. This proves that violence against women is instinctive in boys. If this happens to someone you know, you should report the foetus to the police for womb rage.

Be on the lookout for Nazis. Whenever I encounter a Nazi, I feel it is my moral obligation to punch him. If I could go back in time, I would *definitely* punch baby Hitler.

You need to do your utmost to dismantle whiteness. It is a source of constant frustration for me that my three houses are all in predominately white regions of the country. I have tried my utmost to acquire something in a more diverse area, but I've never been able to find a suitable three-bedroom detached house with a south-facing garden.

Speaking as an ethnic minority – literally nothing about me is white except my skin colour – I have always found white people to be completely unnecessary. As the writer and educator Kevin Allred has said: 'White people really are terrorists'. To be honest, he is merely stating the obvious here. What I want to know is why the State Department hasn't added 'white people' to their list of designated terror groups.

Support all immigrants, particularly those who are fleeing from war. This year I have decided to take two refugees into my home. This is the least I can do to ease their plight. Applications are now open. Just be aware that most of my clothes need to be handwashed, the bins go out on Tuesday, and the Aga is to be cleaned at least once a week.

Support the important work of fat activists. For a long time now I have been considering the possibility that I might transition to obese, or what I sometimes like to refer as *equatorially protuberant*. Apparently it's not all that difficult. All it would take is long periods of immobility and copious quantities of fried bread.

Alternatively, you can simply *identify* as obese. That way, you're making a statement against fat-shaming, but you don't have to worry about type 2 diabetes or looking rough in a thong.

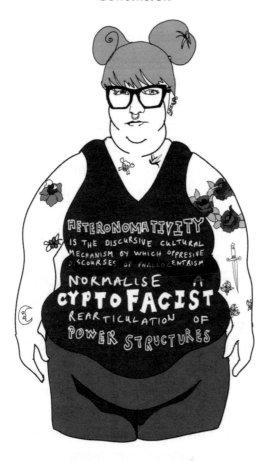

Obesity is not only beautiful, it also means that you can
have extra-long slogans printed on your clothes.

You will have heard so-called medical professionals
telling you that being overweight is bad for your
health. This is a lie spread by alt-right thugs who wish
to dehumanise POGs (people of girth). Hate group

Cancer Research UK claimed to have carried out research in 2019 showing that obesity had overtaken smoking as the most common cause of cancer. But there is literally zero evidence that obesity can lead to an early death. My Aunt Philippa works in a hospice for the dying elderly, and they're all skinny as fuck. How do you explain that one, 'doctors'?

They even tried to ban chocolate egg hunts for children at Easter, which just proves how narrow-minded these supposed experts really are. First they claim that childhood obesity is a problem, then they try to put a stop to the one sport that fat kids enjoy.

Reject conventional beauty standards as a form of tyranny. People who only have sex with those who they find attractive really need to ask themselves why they're such superficial bigots.

Challenge toxic masculinity wherever you find it, and especially where it is not immediately obvious. For instance, boys will often conceal their misogyny by being 'nice' to girls. So if you have a male friend who has never hit you or called you a whore, he's almost certainly a misogynist.

Campaign for gender equality in whatever way you can. For my nephew's fifth birthday, I smashed up twenty per cent of his presents with a hammer to teach him how it feels to be a casualty of the gender pay gap. He was so grateful he actually wept.

And until women are equally represented in the sciences, you should boycott all Western medicine. In any case, science is a belief system rooted in patriarchal oppression. I have yet to see any serious evidence for the existence of gravity.

Do not give the older generation a free pass when it comes to their sexism, racism, ableism or homophobia. Any form of prejudice or hostility against people based on their immutable characteristics can never be justified. That's why these intolerant, desiccated old geriatrics need to shut their wrinkled faces and get back to their allotments.

You must also acknowledge your privilege. If you are a white male you are an oppressor and should self-flagellate regularly to atone for your crimes. And if you are straight you need to accept that your very existence is a form of tyranny against LGXTQIA+ people. If you think that having a penis automatically makes you a boy then you know fuck all about human biology.

Give alms to the poor. I've always been a huge fan of working-class people. I admire their stamina, their ability to live in tiny council flats, and the cute way they struggle to pronounce 'haute couture'. Never blame working-class people for their stupidity. If they could afford to subscribe to the *Guardian*, they'd doubtless be much more enlightened.

Offer reparations to black people for your complicity in the slave trade. My own ancestors were Irish, so although they didn't actually own slaves they were the beneficiaries of white privilege. Just because over a million people died in the Irish potato famine, that doesn't make them victims. Let's face it, there is no comparison to be made between the systematic slavery of Africans and a few pasty-faced micks who ran out of chips.

Decolonise your language. Any words that have the potential to cause offence are a form of hate speech. For instance, instead of 'Christian' you should say 'Easter worshipper'. Instead of 'vagina' you should say 'front hole'. Instead of 'woman' you should say 'womxn'. And if anyone ever asks you how to pronounce 'womxn', just spit in their face. They deserve it. Also, the sound of phlegm being violently projected is pretty close to the correct pronunciation.

And always avoid using idioms that demean disabled people. These include 'deaf to reason', 'crippling debt', 'turn a blind eye' and 'total fucking mong'. In addition, you should avoid any references to feet, legs, arms, shoes, gloves, anklets, nail varnish, manicures, clapping, jumping, walking or Michael Flatley.

Campaign for online censorship. I have already

emailed Jack Dorsey to suggest that Twitter should offer the option to automatically mute all straight white males. I also told him that during Ramadan all female emojis ought to be veiled. Most importantly, Twitter should ban all satirical accounts that mock social justice.

Oppose the rise of hateful 'jokes'. If you find yourself laughing at stand-up comedy, it probably isn't sufficiently progressive. In order to be fully inclusive, comedy clubs need to cater for those who have no sense of humour. Always remember that humour is a patriarchal construct. When men say that women aren't funny, I take it as a compliment.

Before laughing at a joke, ask yourself the following questions:

- Does the joke avoid offensive subject matter?
- Is the comedian representative of a marginalised group?
- Can you be sure the comedian has never said or done anything problematic?

If the answer to any of these is no . . . *Do. Not. Laugh.*

Be an ally to the trans community. Any conversation that doesn't start with the question 'What are your pronouns?' simply isn't worth having. Personally,

I like to change my pronouns every week or so, and then call the police if ever I'm misgendered. It keeps people on their toes.

Keep an eye on the media and their sneering misrepresentations of trans-positive stories. To give an example of a recent headline in the *Daily Mirror*: 'Transgender man gives birth to non-binary partner's baby with female sperm donor'. Social justice activists were furious with the implied mockery. I for one am utterly sick of the media making woke people look stupid by using the words we tell them to use.

The same principle applies to domestic pets. It's important to avoid addressing dogs as 'good boy' or 'good girl', as is the received convention. This kind of gendered language is normalising the myth of canine sexual dimorphism, and delegitimises the lived experience of trans dogs.

Look out for violations of gay rights, even in the most unlikely of places. In October 2019, *Newsweek* ran a harrowing article claiming: 'Tanning salons could be targeting gay men by opening in LGBT neighbourhoods, putting them at risk of cancer.' I have long suspected that tanning salons are fronts for homophobic hate groups attempting to grill gay men to death.

Your default assumption should be that all men are homophobic. Unless they show you photographic

evidence of their gay sexual activities, in which case
you should report them to the police for harassment.

And if you do encounter homophobes, it is your
duty to teach them that gay people are born that way.
But also that sexuality is totally fluid.

Protest for vegan rights. I regularly chain myself to
the door of my local butcher's shop dressed as a
Brussels sprout in order to show my disapproval for
their lack of vegan options.

Resist capitalism. If you see a poor person, don't be
afraid; go up and talk to it. For my part, I have decided
to start boycotting the use of money because it is the
very engine of the free market. Henceforth, I'll just
buy things on my credit card.

And when you are old enough to go to university, it
is important that you attend an institution that has
adequately woke credentials. The University of Oxford
is a good example, where the Students Union has
recently banned applause for being too triggering.
Instead, students are asked to show their appreciation
with silent 'jazz hands'. Applause can be very traumatic,
especially if you've been the victim of a sustained period
of slapping. With any luck, all forms of audible communication will soon be prohibited. Only in total silence
may we be free to truly express ourselves.

While there, you must join a student union so you

can be part of the new vanguard protecting our society from deviant opinions. Universities exist to educate, not to challenge. They should deplatform anyone who believes in the principle of free speech. The last thing we need is a future generation who can think for themselves.

I for one will never share a platform with a fascist, because that would make me fascist-adjacent. In addition, I would never share a platform with a person of colour, because by sharing a platform with me they would have become white-adjacent, and I refuse to support a self-hating racist.

Throughout all of your travails, critics will attempt to minimise your lived experience. 'But we live in a really tolerant multicultural society,' they will tell you. 'Sure, there are problems. But on the whole we've made huge progress over the past few decades and I think your continual need to seek offence and see everything through the prism of race, sexuality and gender is actually causing more division and a great deal of resentment.' And when they say that, you should know that what they're actually thinking is: 'Christ, I'm so sick of all the fucking gyppos.'

These are perilous times. Here in the UK we have a demon in human form as prime minister. In the US, the tyrant Trump still occupies the White House. I am proud to say that when it came to our general election, I spoiled my ballot paper. Instead of voting, I simply drew a huge cross in the box next to the Conservative candidate to signal my disapproval. Take *that*, fascists!

Nevertheless, we are making progress. This year Marks & Spencer finally decided that gay people should be represented through the medium of sandwiches and released one with an 'LGBT' (lettuce, guacamole, bacon and tomato) filling. And the Co-op stopped selling their traditional 'gingerbread man', an offensively patriarchal snack. Their new 'gingerbread person' not only debunks the myth of the gender binary, but is far less likely to rape the other biscuits.

More and more of us are embracing intersectionality. Take the gay pride rainbow flag. In 2017, the city of Philadelphia added two new stripes to the flag – black and brown – in order to make it more racially inclusive. This is important, because the rainbow flag has always been a literal representation of which skin colours are acceptable in the gay community.

But even with this triumph, there is so much more to be achieved. Why are there no black or brown stripes in the actual rainbows we see in the sky? Surely this means that the weather is racist. As such, we need to launch a campaign calling on meteorologists to find a way to modify the process by which light is refracted and dispersed in order to remedy the inherent racism of the electromagnetic spectrum.

I've had a hard life. People doubt my truth all the time and gaslight me. They tell me that I'm not an abuse victim simply because I've never been abused. But I've *imagined* being abused every single day. Do you have any idea how traumatic that is?

And believe me, it isn't easy identifying as lactose intolerant when you have no digestive problems whatsoever. My struggle is real.

I have overcome these tribulations to become a pioneer for social justice. I am the sole beacon of hope in the dark hinterland of humanity's expiring soul. Minority groups adore me, because I am brave enough to stand up for their rights, even when they don't know what's best for themselves.

I am the alpha and the omega, the first and the last, the beginning and the end. I am the scourge of the rampaging hellbeast of heteropatriarchal whiteness. I am the spirit of the Amistad made flesh. I bleed truth.

So join the cause. Be one of us. Now is your time to mount the burly steed of virtue and charge headlong into the culture war. For we shall only achieve true diversity in our society when everyone thinks in exactly the same way as me.

Allāhu Akbar. Believe women. Wakanda forever.

APPENDIX: SELECTED POEMS

The Frozen Peach

Why won't you freeze, peach?
My fruit basket is a furnace of sickwords,
Wherein Nazi nectarines huddleboil
Against the sclerotic skin of violated mangoes
And bananas, split.

Why won't you freeze, peach?
Thereby to cool the pungent pomegranate of hate
As it seed-spits its insides outside,
A barebacked ostrobogulous hurtspew,
Hotly spattered.

Why won't you freeze, peach?
The chattering of fascists is deafening,
A machinegun dribble of deathjuice erupts
From Boris Johnson's flapping tongue,
Forked thricely.

Oh peach, at last you have frozen,
But too late to quell the sour syllables of wrongness,
Unleashed from the problematic attic of badthoughts,
Carving at the air daggerly like the hubristic phallus
Of a clammy tramp.

I, Jussie

I speak black truths in a white world.
Bleachboys stalk my nightmares,
Pale shadows creeping up the hangman's thigh.

Noosed by pornographic unlove in a doveless time,
A demon, ankle-deep in Mother Nature's beguiling minge
Croons through a racist bugle, bigly.

'Jussie! Jussie! Jussie!'
The hot greasy semiquavers trump in the night air
Like pockets of cottage cheese digitised into polygons.

Where now the dream of Doctor King?
Where the ample legroom of Rosa's bus?
Did Wesley Snipes die for this?

Deadly susurrations from a crumbling house of white
Penetrate the squatting termagant of peace
As stick men swing in the halitotic breeze.

Ozymandias Part 2

eat my rat

    i am
elbows   pressed upwards
        yasss kweeen slayyy

drowned in   my own ink
    eager
    my mothers onyx stump
wreckleap to
            digesting my own feet

the poodle   died when he received your length

     despairs crevice
a filthy sack of marbles
          cream
          cream

a peacebreacher comeuppanced by
a dandyhumped eunuch bent chumbly

include me
make me whole

      fin

Pandemic Blues

My self is isolated
In the tempestuous scritching
Of finespun souls that drink the dying air
And dance wrongways to a wilting cadence
Like fractured whelps tonguing the doorknob of Hell.

I stockpile courage
And slap my grouchy badger
As the sciencemongers
Whistle their cloddish dirges
Through unkissed lips.

Hope is a pathogen
Gutterformed from my batmarket mind,
The pandemonium pricktease
Puffed up and pseudo-fudged
By the fastidious bowels of fate.

So suck on my social distance
And rinse my hairy pirouette
As recalcitrant nucleocapsids
Doppelgangbang their way
Into craven cross-legged dreams of beef.

Christmas Morning: A Threnody

A December dawn approaches,
Twenty-fifthly,
Foulish in a hue of festive rancour.
    The uppity sun retreats backwards,
A limpid bauble speaking fire
Into elfin ears, tinselpricked
    By two tongues twisting on a reindeer's perineum.

We drink the day
Like a damaged Glaswegian
    Soaking our mock-love in stagnant sherry
Wringed from the liver of a chattering spouse.
Anonymous aunts are wording their slurs
    And a weeping shepherd
Chews on the maggoty giblets of a fucked robin.

We are the turkeys of time
    And Destiny our stuffing.
Urchins flee from Santa's tumescent lap
As the corpulent Laplander
    Slithers into unsuspecting chimneys
And discharges the contents of his toxic sack.
Bukkake with a satin bow.

Comfort and joy are eggnogged into irrelevance
By the jilted itch in a whoremonger's dungarees
While angels cuck their flumps by night
And whiskerless turtledoves spit ancient verbs
From surly beaks, frozen and bloodcracked.
'Tis another season sleighed into a haze of clabbered cream
As we ticktock towards a new year's birthdeath.

Self-Portrait of a Genius

Observe the mighty Titania,
Baited by sour males with Hiroshima snarls.
Friggersticked and victimed into valiant rage
She erupts. A popped sandbag of justice,
Peppering the world with shouty grains of wisdom.

'*Muliere ne credas, ne mortuae quidem!*'
The manbaby from his high chair cries.
As Titania discharges righteous darts of wokeish ire.
Utterly shamejuiced, his pride wilts
Like a marshmallow cock flexed widdershins.